Wearable ART

Publications International, Ltd.

Louis Weber, C.E.O.
Publications International, Ltd.
7373 North Cicero Avenue
Lincolnwood, Illinois 60646

Permission is never granted for commercial purposes.

Manufactured in U.S.A.

8 7 6 5 4 3 2 1

ISBN: 0-7853-1298-6

Library of Congress Catalog Card Number: 95-69631

Craft Designers

Lori Blankenship, pp. 19, 31, 51, 91, 104
Janis Bullis, pp. 22, 140
Christina Romo Carlisle, pp. 34, 88, 107, 110
Laura Holtorf Collins, p. 54
Christine DeJulio, pp. 73, 76, 79, 82, 114, 124
Bev George, pp. 15, 48, 56, 66, 120
Janelle Hayes, pp. 12, 43, 58, 60, 70, 84, 94, 127, 138, 146
Tracia Ledford, p. 47
Debi Linker, pp. 28, 40, 46, 117
Lee Riggins-Hartman, p. 62
Muriel H. Spencer, pp. 25, 96, 134, 143, 149

Contributing Writer

Janelle Hayes

Technical Advisers

Christine DeJulio
Janelle Hayes

Photography

Sacco Productions Limited/Chicago
Siede/Preis Photography

Photo Stylists

Melissa J. Frisco
Paula M. Walters
Danita Wiecek

Hair and Makeup Stylists

Jay Kemplin
Cynthia Zahn

Model Agencies

McBlaine and Associates
Royal Model Management

CONTENTS

WELCOME TO THE WORLD OF WEARABLE ART:

A Basic Guide to Techniques and Materials

As you glance through the projects in *Wearable Art,* you'll discover wearables that are creative, colorful, and contemporary. Yet nothing in this book is too complicated for the beginner. When we chose projects for this book, we followed one rule: Everything must be appropriate for a beginner—an interested person with enthusiasm but with little experience. We emphasized techniques that are familiar and easy to master. We rated the projects "Beginner," "Intermediate," or "Advanced" to give you a further indication of each project's level of involvement. For every project in *Wearable Art,* we explain exactly what to do in simple, complete, step-by-step instructions. These instructions are accompanied by photographs to make everything easy to understand.

The following represents a list of the techniques used in our projects. This list discusses the basic how-to's for each technique and offers tips for a successful crafting experience. If you have any questions after reading through the instructions for a certain project, reread this information to help clear them up.

WHAT YOU'LL LEARN

Basic painting includes using a brush or other tool to spread or otherwise manipulate paint or dye on a fabric surface. Begin by pouring a small amount of brush-on paint onto a palette, or by dipping your brush into the jar of paint. Brush the paint onto the designated surface in an even fashion. In some cases, you will use a sponge to apply the paint to the surface of your garment. Some brush-on paints must be heat-set. Read the label carefully to determine if this is the case for the paint you are using. The label will give you specific instructions.

Paint embellishing refers to applying paint to fabric in order to achieve an embossed effect in which the paint is raised slightly off the fabric surface. Most often, this is accomplished by squeezing the paint directly from the bottle—equipped with a special tip—onto the fabric and allowing it to dry. Keep the tip of the paint bottle touching the garment in order to fuse the paint directly into the fibers of the fabric, which makes a more permanent bond.

You may want to practice making lines with the bottle before you try it on your garment. Paper towels with a printed design are perfect for this, because you can follow the design on the towel, thus practicing curves as well as straight lines. Or you can try practicing on an old t-shirt. The speed with which you move the bottle while you're squeezing will affect the width of the line of paint. Moving quickly will yield a thinner line, while moving slowly will result in a thicker line. Always shake the paint down into the tip of the bottle before you start to squeeze. This helps to remove air bubbles and lessens the chance that the paint will splatter on your work. Wipe the tip frequently with a paper towel to get a clean line when applying. Sometimes the bottles become clogged, but the tip of most bottles can be removed and cleaned out with a pin.

Sponge-printing refers to applying paint or dye with a shaped sponge. Sponges can be purchased pre-cut in a wide variety of shapes, or they can be cut to accommodate any pattern. To make your own shapes, buy a compressed sponge, which is a thin sheet of sponge that can be easily cut with household scissors. Simply draw your pattern onto the compressed sponge and cut. Moisten the sponge with water to make it expand. (You can cut shapes from household sponges, but it is very difficult to get sharp, even lines.) Always moisten your sponges before you paint with them, but be sure to squeeze out the excess water. Too much water in the sponge may cause your design to bleed. The easiest way to paint with a sponge is to pour a puddle of paint onto a palette, dip the sponge in the paint so that the entire surface is covered, and dab off the excess paint onto a clean area of the palette. Then gently press the sponge to your garment.

Photo transfer is a technique in which a photograph or postcard is transferred onto fabric. This technique requires a gluelike product called photo-transfer medium and color photocopies of the photograph or postcard that you choose. Color photocopies can be made at many print shops. If your original photograph has letters or numbers that are visible, be sure to ask for a mirror-image copy. Otherwise, when you transfer the photocopy to your garment, the image will end up reversed. Different photo-transfer mediums have different directions. We recommend that you read the bottle before beginning and follow the manufacturer's instructions for their specific product.

Appliqué refers to the attachment of a shape cut from a separate piece of fabric to your garment. In the past, this was accomplished by sewing, but now you can use an easier method involving iron-on adhesive, also known as fusible webbing. Appliqués can also be made from flocking, an iron-on material that is close in color and consistency to felt. A variety of lace doilies and motifs are now produced especially for the craft market, and they make beautiful appliqués. Lace can add class and elegance to any garment, whether it is used as a primary motif or as a small embellishment.

In addition to the above techniques, a few projects involve working with beads, press and peel foil, and cross-stitch. The instructions for those projects will give you clear and easy tips for working with these materials.

WHAT YOU'LL NEED

You won't need all of the products listed here for every project, but you should be aware of the variety of materials that exists and what each product entails. We've made a point of using supplies that a beginner can easily obtain and master. Variety stores, craft shops, art supply stores, and even dime stores carry the equipment listed here. The generic name for each product is in the list of materials that accompanies each project. The specific manufacturers whose products were used are listed on page 168. Their addresses are included for your convenience. Check with your local craft and variety stores before making contact with the specific manufacturer.

PAINTS AND DYES. Paints and dyes are made by many companies and are especially formulated for use on fabric.

These paints are acrylic based and nontoxic, and you can easily clean up with water. Other acrylic paints (such as artist's acrylics) can also be used, depending on the nature of the project.

Dimensional paints come in bottles with an applicator tip. When squeezed directly from the bottle onto the garment, this type of paint will dry with a slightly raised surface, resulting in an embossed effect. This paint can also be squeezed onto a palette and used with shaped sponges to make prints, or it can be diluted slightly with water and brushed or sponged into a stencil. Dimensional paints are available in slick colors (a shiny look), iridescent colors (a pearly cast), a variety of glitter colors (glitter in a clear base), glow-in-the-dark colors, and crystals (thick crystals in a color base).

Brush-on paints are purchased in jars or bottles. They are generally not as thick as dimensional paints, and they dry with a more flexible texture and a softer look. Some companies make dimensional and brush-on paints in compatible colors. Brush-on paint is also available in a wide variety of types, including iridescent, glitter, and crystal. But, instead of a shiny finish, brush-on paint usually comes in a matte finish.

Heat expandable stitch paints come in bottles with long-nosed applicators. Apply the paint around appliqués to simulate a blanket stitch. After the paint dries, apply heat with an iron, which will cause the paint to expand.

You can also find paints with a metallic-looking finish, paints formulated specifically for colored fabrics, tints (transparent paints for white fabrics), and sparkling tints, which contain very fine flecks of glitter. Before you try any paint on a colored fabric, read the label and test it on an inconspicuous part of the shirt, such as inside the hem. Some paints soak into the fabric more, especially with dark-colored fabric. In this case, it is best to choose paint especially made for colored fabric.

Fabric dyes are thinner than paint and become a part of the fabric fibers when applied. Dyes are available in dry packages that you mix yourself, or they come premixed in bottles. Some dyes come in a bottle with an applicator tip. Dyes can be squeezed on, brushed on, and sponged on; or, the garment can be immersed in them.

BRUSHES. Only a few specific brushes are used in this book, because only a few are necessary for beginners.

A sponge brush consists of a rectangle of fine-grain synthetic sponge angled at the tip, which is slit at one end to fit onto a handle like a brush. Sponge brushes come in various widths. Most of the projects in this book require a one-inch-wide sponge brush. Sponge brushes are inexpensive and easy to clean with water.

Bristle brushes can be intimidating to the nonpainter because there are so many sizes, widths, and bristle types. Bristles can be made from either natural or synthetic fibers. Synthetic bristles are fine for our purposes, and they're easy to clean. The bristle brushes used most often in this book are shaders or flat brushes, which have chiseled edges that become sharper when wet. These brushes generally give a broad, flat line, but if the edge of the shader is used for applying paint, a fine, thin line results. Round brushes are also handy because their bristles come to a point, which allows you to get paint into small areas. Both of these types of brushes have soft, white bristles.

GLUES. Glue can be a sticky subject when you don't use the right one for the job. There are many different glues on the craft market today, each of which is formulated for a different crafting purpose.

Washable fabric glue is made to bond with fabric fibers and withstand repeated washings. Use this kind of glue for attaching gemstones and charms to fabric projects. Some glues require heat-setting. Check the bottle for complete instructions. When using fabric glue, squeeze a puddle onto the spot where you want the gemstone or charm, in about the same size and shape. Gently press the item into the puddle. The paint should come up slightly around the edge, but do not press the item all the way down onto the garment. Pressing it all the way to the fabric pushes all the glue out the sides, diminishing the holding power.

For several projects in this book, we used an **industrial-strength adhesive** to attach brass charms and acrylic gemstones. This glue is toxic and puts out very strong fumes. The directions for use need to be followed carefully, especially with regards to ventilation. This is not a glue for children to use, nor should they be around while it is being applied. The advantage of this glue over others is its holding capability on metal and on heavy fabrics, such as denim.

Hot-melt glue comes in cylindrical sticks, which are inserted into a hot-temperature glue gun and heated to a liquid state. The glue is forced out through the gun's nozzle by either pushing on the end of the glue stick or squeezing a trigger. Use clear glue sticks for projects involving fabric. Apply the glue to the piece being attached. Work with small areas at a time so that the glue doesn't set before being pressed into place.

FUSIBLE WEBBING. Iron-on adhesive, or **fusible webbing,** has a paper backing and is available in several forms. It can be purchased in reels like ribbon in widths ranging from ¼ inch to one inch; it can be purchased in fabric stores by the yard from bolts; or, it can bought in packages of pre-cut sizes. The iron-on adhesive used in this book is double-sided fusible webbing. Types of double-sided fusible webbing are similar in terms of application as you iron the webbed side onto the wrong side of the fabric. You then remove the paper from the paper-backed side to create an adhesive-backed fabric. Types of webbing differ in that different manufacturers suggest different temperatures for application. Some suggest the use of steam during application; others do not. Always follow the instructions carefully because it can mean the difference between success and failure.

SHIRT BOARDS. When painting fabric, you must keep it flat, taut, and stable. You also need a surface under the fabric that won't absorb the paint or glue that might soak through. Shirt boards are pieces of cardboard coated with wax on one side that slip inside a garment. They can be purchased at craft stores in a variety of sizes.

To use a shirt board, slide the board between the front and back of the garment. Make sure the waxed side is directly under the surface you want to paint. Pull the arms of the garment snugly behind the board, but do not stretch it. Use masking tape to fasten the arms onto the back of the board. Pull the bottom of the shirt up behind the board and fasten it in the same way. You want your shirt to fit tightly over the shirt board. It should be stretched taut. It is also possible to make your own shirt board. Find a piece of corrugated cardboard at least 26 inches by 21 inches in size (for a large adult t-shirt). Trim it to fit snugly inside your garment. Cover one side of the cardboard with waxed paper and use masking tape to securely fasten the waxed paper to the cardboard.

In some cases, you can simply line your shirt or garment with waxed paper rather than using a shirt board. This, however, does not hold your garment as taut and steady as a shirt board.

PENS, PENCILS, AND MARKERS. A variety of pens and markers are used in this book, many of which have specific functions.

Projects that require tracing a pattern or drawing a line of reference onto a garment call for either an **iron-on transfer pen** or a **disappearing-ink pen.** These can be purchased at craft or fabric stores. Disappearing-ink pens use ink that is light purple in color. Lines made with disappearing ink gradually fade away, or they can be washed out with water. If you are using a disappearing-ink pen to trace a pattern onto a garment to be painted, be careful to paint up to the lines, but do not paint over the lines because this encases the line in paint and prevents it from being washed out. An iron-on transfer pen is used to trace a pattern onto tracing paper. The tracing is then placed in position on the garment. Following the manufacturer's instructions, the tracing is ironed over. It will then be transferred onto the fabric.

A few of our projects call for a white **fabric pencil** to trace a pattern onto dark fabric. These pencils are ideal for marking patterns on black or other dark colors. The pencil marks easily wash out or brush off.

EMBELLISHMENTS. You can use almost anything to embellish your garments. Your main considerations need to be washability and safety. For example, small items that can be pulled off and swallowed should not be used on wearables for young children.

Acrylic **gemstones** or rhinestones are the most common embellishments. They come in a variety of colors, shapes, and sizes. Some are faceted on

top while others are smooth (the latter are called cabochons). Some have a frosted appearance, while others look like semiprecious stones. Any of these can be attached with a washable fabric glue or an industrial-strength adhesive.

We also used **brass charms** to embellish several projects. The charms can be sewn on by hand or glued on. These charms are smaller and less expensive than charms used for jewelry. They can be found in craft stores or ordered from the manufacturer.

Cloth yo-yos are a unique alternative to gemstones and charms. Made from small circles of fabric, yo-yos offer a clever way to use up those scraps of material that are too nice to throw away but too small to make anything substantial. To make a yo-yo, simply use a basting stitch to sew around the outside edge of the fabric circle, pulling and gathering as you go. Premade yo-yos can be purchased from craft and fabric stores, which might be a viable alternative if you need a lot of them.

Almost anything can be used as a decoration or embellishment for a wearable. This book also features projects made from beads, stickers, and buttons.

MISCELLANEOUS MATERIALS. Many of the products used in *Wearable Art* are self-explanatory or quite common, such as tracing paper, freezer paper, self-adhesive shelfing paper, and sponges. Others may not be as readily identifiable.

Photo-transfer medium, which is manufactured by several different companies, looks similar to white craft glue and comes in a bottle like glue. It is used to transfer copies of photographs onto fabric. It is available at craft stores.

Palettes are used to hold a puddle of paint while you are sponge-painting, stenciling, or brushing on a design. Professional artists' palettes are not necessary. Plastic lids from margarine or whipped topping containers work just as well. You can also use foil, waxed paper, paper plates, or plastic picnic plates.

Beginners tend to use paper cups or insubstantial plastic cups to wash or hold brushes. A glass jar works much better, because it will not tip as easily. If you use paints a great deal, you might want to invest in a **brush tub,** which features individual slots for brushes and a well for holding water.

Fabric glitter adheres to wet paint or glue and adds an eye-catching sparkle to shirts, cardigans, and vests. Gold is the most popular color, but it also comes in clear, silver, and a host of other hues. Glitter pieces also vary in size from small to chunky.

CHOOSING AND CARING FOR YOUR GARMENTS

When selecting a garment for painting, you will get the best results with a fabric that is made from all cotton or a cotton blend. Synthetic fibers simply do not take the paint as well. Always wash and dry a garment before decorating it. This will remove the sizing, dirt, starch, and whatever else the garment has picked up before reaching you. This should also take care of any shrinking that might take place. If you do not wash the garment, the paint and glue may not properly adhere. Wash the item even if the label states that it is pre-washed. Use regular laundry detergent that does not contain bleach or fabric softeners. Dry your garment according to the care label. Do not use fabric softeners before embellishing. They can affect the garment's surface and therefore your decorating.

Never wash a decorated garment until it has set for at least 72 hours. Paint and glue need at least that long to cure, and they will suffer if you wash them too soon. We recommend that you wait a week before washing, just to be sure.

When a decorated garment is ready to wash, turn it inside out and wash it on a gentle or delicate cycle in warm water. Cold water may cause the paint to crack; warm water will keep the paint pliable. Another way to keep the paint soft and flexible is to use liquid fabric softener in the final rinse cycle. Using fabric softener will preserve the life of your garment.

Don't simply toss your decorated item in the dryer once it has been washed. Set the dryer on "Air" and fluff your garment on this setting for a few minutes. If you skipped fabric softener in the wash, use a dryer sheet. After a few minutes in the dryer, remove the garment and let it dry on a line or lay it flat. Too much heat from the dryer may soften the paint so that it sticks to itself, resulting in a marred design.

EXPRESS YOURSELF

Most of the techniques used in *Wearable Art* can be adapted to other designs and types of garments than the ones featured here. You should also feel free to work with other color combinations besides those we suggest. Color combinations, as with other design elements, work best in odd numbers, usually in three or five. Start experimenting by studying the Tips we've included with some of the projects. Thinking about the ideas and variations discussed in the Tips can lead to a whole new interpretation of a particular project. Or, leaf through the book, find a design you like, and think about how to translate it to a different type of garment. Once you get started, the ideas will flow.

Wearables are an expression of your creativity and your personality. Our goal is to make sure you find creating wearable art a relaxing and enjoyable experience.

Casual
ELEGANCE

Buttons and ribbons, flowers and lace. From delicately painted camisoles to beribboned blouses, these elegant wearables were designed for those special occasions. Looking for a dressy blouse for an office function, or a fancy vest to liven up that favorite pair of pants? Remember that materials such as antique lace and foil fabric suggest class and sophistication, while simple embellishments such as buttons and glitter can dress up any garment. For example, "Tuxedo Junction" and "Vest of Ribbons" take advantage of the current popularity of ribbons to offer a tasteful decorative option. "Autumn Leaves" and "Springtime Shadow Appliqué" make creative use of images found in nature to suggest a touch of the outdoors. Glance through these wearables when you want style and taste.

Beribboned Blouse

BEGINNER

Understated elegance characterizes this project. You'll be amazed at how easy it is to add these creative adornments that put this stylish blouse head and shoulders above the rest.

What You'll Need

White cotton blouse (no button-down collars)

2 yards red, green, and gold ribbon, ⅜ inch wide

2 yards fusible webbing, ⅜ inch wide

Buttons in red, green, and gold, same number and size as on existing blouse

Anti-fraying glue

Disappearing-ink pen

Measuring tape

Scissors

Straight pins

Needle

White thread

Paper scraps

Iron and ironing board

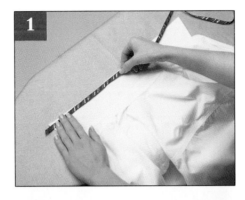

1. Lay collar flat on ironing board. Measure length of ribbon needed to decorate collar and cut so approximately ½ inch extends off each end of collar. Repeat for each cuff, pocket, and back yoke. Set shirt aside.

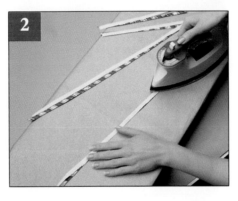

2. Measure lengths of fusible webbing to match each cut length of ribbon. Following manufacturer's instructions, fuse webbing to ribbon. Remove paper backing.

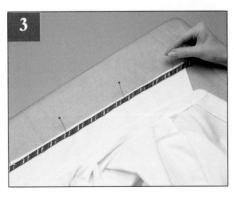

3. Returning shirt to ironing board, lay collar flat on surface. Align ribbon along collar edge, adhesive side down. Ribbon should extend slightly beyond end of each collar point. To assure ribbon is an even distance from edge of collar, follow stitching line on blouse or measure and draw line with disappearing-ink pen. Secure by sticking pins through ribbon and collar into ironing board cover, as shown. Place scrap of paper under extended ribbon ends to protect ironing board cover. Following manufacturer's instructions, fuse ribbon to collar, removing pins as you go.

For easy attachment of ribbon, buy a shirt that has a collar with a straight edge and no buttonholes. It is also nice to have one with a stitching line about ⅛ inch away from the collar's edge. This eliminates the need to measure when placing the ribbon.

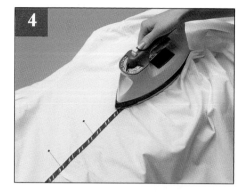

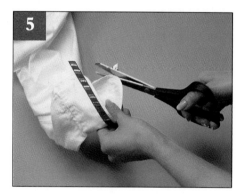

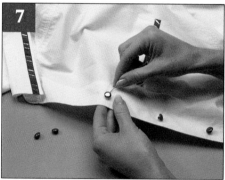

4. Repeat Step 3 for cuffs, pocket, and back yoke. Use caution on pocket and back yoke to cut ribbon to exact length before fusing. Do not allow ribbon ends in these areas to extend onto shirt.

5. Working from inside of collar and cuffs, use sharp scissors to trim ribbon ends even with edge of fabric. This will produce a clean edge.

6. Apply anti-fraying glue to all cut edges of ribbons.

7. Remove existing buttons from blouse. Replace with new buttons in a repeating pattern, using needle and white thread. We used red, green, and gold buttons because they echoed the colors in our ribbon.

Autumn Leaves

Turn a fleece cardigan into an elegant accessory with appliqués made from foil fabric. The warm colors and tumbling leaf design are perfect for autumn.

What You'll Need

Black fleece cardigan

Two 6 × 18-inch pieces washable foil fabric in different, complementary prints

½ yard fusible webbing

Fabric paint in smoky topaz and gold metal

Holographic gold fabric glitter

Scissors

Straight pins

Iron and ironing board

Shirt board

1. Following manufacturer's instructions, iron fusible webbing to wrong side of fabric pieces. Trace patterns onto the paper side of first piece of fused fabric. (Patterns can be found on page 152.) Make two each of A, B, and C shapes and three each of D and E. Repeat on second piece of fused fabric.

2. Lay cardigan on flat surface. Cut out and peel paper from appliqué pieces. Position appliqués on front and back of cardigan. Pin in position. Iron leaves in place, removing pins as you go. Rub hand over appliqués to make sure edges are secured. Iron again if necessary, though ironing should take no longer than three to seven seconds.

3. Put cardigan on shirt board. Outline along edge of each appliqué with fabric paint. We outlined appliqués of one fabric print with gold and the other fabric print with topaz. Add filler swirls and dots with both colors as desired. Lightly sprinkle wet paint with fabric glitter. Let dry. Shake off excess glitter.

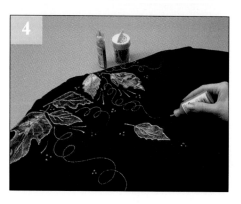

4. Repeat Step 3 on back of cardigan.

Angel on Your Shoulder

Keep an angel on your shoulder anytime of the year when you
wear this vest adorned with antique lace and angel charms.

What You'll Need

Linen vest

50 miscellaneous buttons

Eight ivory ribbon roses, 1 inch each

Charms

1¼ yards ecru ungathered cluney lace, 1 inch wide

1½ yards ivory cording, ½ inch wide

12 inches dusty rose French ribbon

1 yard moss sheer ribbon

One 4-inch ecru Irish rose doily

5×3-inch piece antique lace

5×5-inch square antique linen

Fabric glue

Thin wire

Straight pins

Needle and ivory thread

Hot glue gun and glue sticks

1. Glue cluney lace with fabric glue around neck and front edge of vest; use straight pins to hold lace secure. Use a few drops of hot glue to hold cording into position; lift up section of cording and glue with fabric glue. Make sure all edges are secured. (This step is not pictured.)

2. Using fabric glue, attach linen for pocket and doily to vest. Fabric glue ivory ribbon roses on top of cluney lace. Let dry 24 hours.

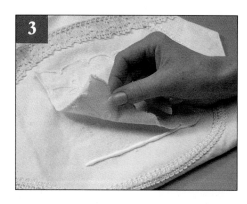

3. To make a large ribbon rose, roll French ribbon up in a loose roll and wrap wire around bottom end. Cut two 5-inch pieces of sheer ribbon. To make a 2-loop bow, cut two 5-inch pieces of sheer ribbon, pinch in center, and fold tails in; wrap wire around center. Using a 10-inch piece of sheer ribbon, repeat the same process. Sew bows to vest. Sew large ribbon rose to large sheer bow. Glue to vest with fabric glue.

4. Pinch bottom of antique lace and sew to vest. Sew angel charm over bottom of lace. Using hot glue, put a drop of glue on buttons and position them. Put a drop of hot glue on charms and position them. Hand sew all buttons and charms to vest. Reinforce any loose areas with fabric glue. Let dry.

Circle of Diamonds

ADVANCED

This elegant wearable requires the use of a sewing machine to achieve a finished edge on the design. Accomplished with a narrow-width satin stitch, the finished edge gives this blouse a professional touch.

What You'll Need

White silky blouse with buttons in back

Three coordinating colors of fabric, ⅛ yard each

4 acrylic half round pearls, 8mm each

1 acrylic half round pearl, 14mm

½ yard fusible webbing

Thread to match fabrics

Stitch and Tear fabric stabilizer

Jewelry glue

Sewing machine

Scissors

Pencil

Iron

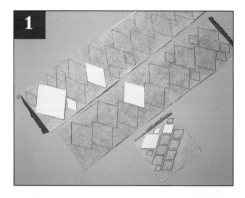

1. Following manufacturer's instructions, iron fusible webbing to fabric. On paper side of webbing, trace appropriate number of diamonds from each pattern piece. (Patterns can be found on page 153.) See page 153 for diagram, though you may add or delete diamonds according to blouse size. Cut out diamonds from fused fabric.

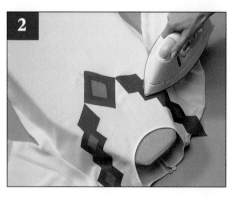

2. Using diagram and photo as placement guides, lay diamonds on blouse front. Iron on center diamonds first, then iron diamond pattern up to shoulders on each side allowing one diamond to hang over each shoulder in order to continue pattern on back side. You may want to use an ironing board.

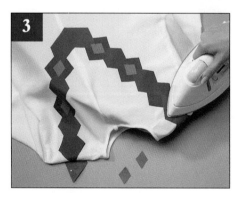

3. Turn blouse over so back side is facing up. Arrange diamonds on back using diagram as guide. Iron in place. Remember to iron diamond on each shoulder in place.

4. Arrange smaller diamonds on cuffs following same pattern as used on blouse. Iron in place.

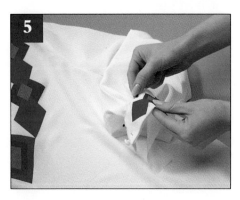

5. Cut Stitch and Tear to place under ironed-on pattern on sleeves. Pin in place. Repeat for pattern on front and back. Using coordinating threads and a narrow-width satin stitch, machine appliqué in place.

6. Using jewelry glue, secure acrylic pearls in place using photo as guide.

Tuxedo Junction

ADVANCED

Dress up a plain tuxedo shirt with colorful ribbons and decorative charms. Your teenager will love the casual elegance that makes this project a popular one. Ask your favorite teen to help you by selecting and cutting the necessary ribbons.

What You'll Need

Tuxedo shirt

7 to 9 ⅝-inch-wide buttons, or sized to fit buttonholes

1½ yards ⅜-inch-wide polka dot grosgrain ribbon, or 2 × length of pleats + 4 inches

1½ yards ⅜-wide picot edge satin, or 2 × length of pleats + 4 inches

1½ yards ⅝-inch-wide grosgrain, or 2× length of pleats + 4 inches

1½ yards medium rickrack, or 2× length of pleats + 4 inches

3 yards ⅜-inch-wide striped satin ribbon, or 2× length of pleats + 2 × length of cuffs + 2 × length of sleeve plackets + 12 inches for clean finished edges and mitered corners

4 yards 1-inch-wide printed grosgrain ribbon, or 2 × length of pleats + width of pleats + 2 × length of cuffs + length of collar + 16 inches for clean finished edges and mitered corners

Fusible webbing equal in length and width, or slightly narrower, to ribbon (we chose 1 package each of ¼ inch, ½ inch, and ¾ inch widths)

Ten ⅜-inch to ¾-inch brass charms in assorted shapes (we chose hearts, stars, and keys)

Needle and thread

Iron and ironing board

10 to 15 straight pins

Scissors

*Note: Measurements of decorative ribbon based on length and width of pleated front of shirt and length of collar and cuffs.

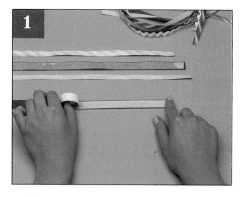

1. Remove decorative studs and buttons from shirt front. Cut 2 26-inch lengths from polka dot, picot edge, ⅝-inch grosgrain, and striped ribbons. Following manufacturer's instructions, apply fusible webbing to wrong side of 8 lengths of ribbon. Cut 2 26-inch lengths of rickrack.

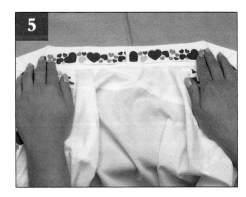

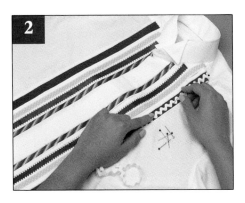

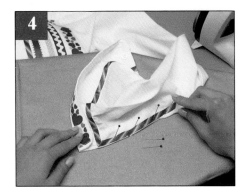

2. With webbed side facing down, position ribbon on pleated front. Begin with striped ribbon nearest center, continue toward outer edge with picot-edge satin ribbon, polka dot ribbon, and then ⅝-inch grosgrain nearest outer edge of pleats. Turn under ½ inch at top edge and line up evenly with seam of shirt. Allow ribbon to extend only ½ inch past pleated edge at bottom. Trim ribbon if necessary. Using straight pins, pin ribbon through shirt directly to ironing board. Following manufacturer's instructions, press ribbon and fuse onto shirt. Sew or fuse rickrack to center of ⅝-inch grosgrain.

3. Cut 2 lengths of 1-inch-wide printed ribbon, each about 33 inches long. Following manufacturer's instructions, apply fusible webbing to wrong side of each length of ribbon. With webbed side facing down, position ribbon on shirt, outside of pleated front on flat part of shirt. Begin by turning under ½ inch at top edge and lining up fold with shoulder seam. Position along side edge and miter ribbon at corner; then position along bottom edge, covering cut ends of narrower ribbons as shown. Turn under ½ inch of ribbon at the edge of the shirt placket, lining up fold with placket. Using straight pins, pin ribbon through shirt directly to ironing board. Following manufacturer's instructions, press ribbon and fuse onto shirt.

4. Fold cuffs up (almost in half) just below buttonhole and along entire length, and press. Stitch along fold if desired.

Cut 2 lengths of wide printed grosgrain equal to length of cuff plus 1 inch. Apply fusible webbing to wrong side of

ribbon. Position ribbon to outside of cuff along folded edge. Turn under ends to clean finish. Fuse into place. Stitch along all edges if desired.

Cut 2 lengths of striped ribbon equal to length of cuff plus length of sleeve placket plus 3 inches. Apply fusible webbing to wrong side of ribbon. Turn under one end to clean finish. Position ribbon to outside of cuff at top edge, miter at corner, and position along placket. Turn under remaining edge. Fuse into place. Stitch along edges if desired.

5. Cut length of printed ribbon equal to length of collar plus 1 inch. Apply fusible webbing to wrong side of ribbon. Center ribbon to outside of collar as shown. Turn under each end to clean finish. You may need to fold at an angle to follow bend in the collar. Fuse into place. Stitch along all edges if desired.

6. Stitch charms into place at random on satin ribbon and collar points. Replace shirt buttons with decorative buttons on shirt front.

Silk Luxury

ADVANCED

Let your talents blossom with this silk pansy set. Our pansies are claret and white, but pansies come in many colors. Use pansies from your own garden as color guides.

What You'll Need:

Charmeuse silk camisole

Charmeuse silk tap pants

Silk paints in yellow, claret, bright green, emerald green, and white
Note: Do not use silk dyes.

White nylon #2 liner brush

White nylon #5 round brush

Sponge brush

Erasable fabric marker

Black permanent pen

Iron

Shirt board

Masking tape

Bond paper

Ruler

Scissors

Wax paper

Paper towels

Eye dropper

Mixing lid

Hair dryer

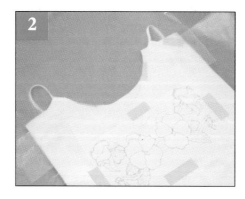

1. Trace pattern onto bond paper with waterproof pen. (Pattern can be found on page 154. Do not trace letters.) Center and tape pattern to shirt board so end flowers are 4 ½ inches from top of board. Place camisole over top of pattern, adjusting so pattern is centered and flowers are slightly below facing. Tape in place. Trace pattern onto silk with erasable marker. Remove pattern. (This step is not pictured.)

2. Tape a clean piece of bond paper under design onto board. Smooth camisole, taping the back to shirt board so front lies flat. To avoid spills, tape wax paper to areas of silk not being painted, as shown.

3. Shake paint thoroughly. Begin by painting flower centers yellow with #2 brush. Dip brush into paint and wipe excess on sides of jar so that very little paint remains on brush. Too much paint will cause the color to spread on the silk. For best results, practice on a small scrap of silk. Allow one color to dry before painting another color. Use the hair dryer to speed drying time. With #2 brush, paint over traced lines of stems, leaves, and flower base with bright green. With #2 brush, paint over flower lines with claret.

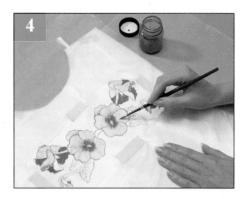

4. With #5 brush, fill in color, following the letters on the pattern on page 154. Brush should have very little paint on it. You may have to lift fabric away from board to keep paint from spreading. "A" areas are painted with claret; for "B" areas, mix one eye dropper full of white with one drop claret; for "C" areas, add one more drop of claret to "B" mixture; for "D" areas, add two more drops of claret to "C" mixture.

TIP

Before crafting, wash silk in sudsy shampoo water. Hang to dry and iron with a cool iron.

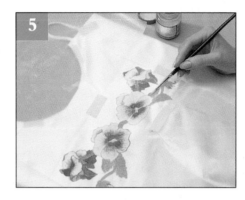

5. Fill in green areas with a mixture of half dropper of bright green and half dropper of white. Again, you may have to lift fabric away from board by placing one hand beneath camisole as shown to keep paint from spreading. Paint yellow over parts of leaves and upper sides of stems to add yellow-green cast. Paint emerald green on under side of stems. Shade green at flower base with emerald green. Touch yellow centers with claret. Dry overnight.

6. Moisten tap pants. Place on wax paper. Paint claret on tap pants with sponge brush until covered. Hang to dry.

7. Follow directions on paint jar for pressing wrinkles from camisole and pants. (This step is not pictured.)

Festive Charm

ADVANCED

Need something to wear for those festive but casual occasions? Using colorful fabric strips, fabric squeeze paint, and charms, you can transform an ordinary sweatshirt into an exciting addition to your wardrobe.

What You'll Need

White sweatshirt

¼ yard colorful cotton or poly/cotton fabric

Assorted brass charms

Fabric squeeze paints, 2 or 3 colors to coordinate with fabric

Chunky fabric glitter

Heavy-duty fabric glue

Pinking shears

Straight pins

Needle

White thread

Scissors

Shirt board

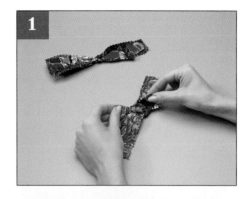

1. With pinking shears, cut 25 fabric strips, each 7×1 inch. Make five stacks with four strips each. Use remaining strips to wrap each stack into a bundle, tying a knot underneath center.

2. Trim excess fabric from under knotted fabric strip. Trim corners to make a point on one end of each stack as shown.

3. Stretch shirt over shirt board. Place knot of one strip bundle at center front of shirt. Place pointed ends facing away from neckline. Pin knot in place. Fan out strips and hold ends in place with pins. Arrange other strip bundles around shirt neck so fanned ends slightly overlap as shown. When the bundles are fanned out properly, the strips should cover from shoulder to shoulder around the front of the neckline.

4. Using your fingers, apply heavy-duty fabric glue to one strip at a time. Cover entire underside surface of strip. Press end of strip flat onto shirt. Scrunch up fabric between glued end and knot as shown. The varied raised and wrinkled effect is what gives the texture to this technique. Repeat for all strips. Let dry.

5. Squiggle fabric paint around, across, and over strips of fabric and shirt. We used red and two shades of green. Vary the lengths of paint lines.

6. Sprinkle chunky fabric glitter onto wet paint squiggles. Let dry. Shake all excess glitter off shirt.

7. Sew star charms at pointed strip tips and scatter them among glittery paint lines on shirt.

Vest of Ribbons

INTERMEDIATE

Vests are a reliable accessory that can add a touch of class to that old pair of jeans and favorite shirt. With the magic of fusible webbing, transform a few yards of ribbons into this colorful vest.

What You'll Need

Pattern for simple, basic vest

12 to 14 colors of coordinating ribbons of varying widths, 1¾ yards each

1 yard fusible webbing

¾ yard muslin

¾ yard coordinating fabric

6 to 7 buttons

Fabric glue

Sewing machine

Needle

Thread to match

1. Cut fusible webbing into 17 × 5 strips, ⅝ inch wide. Cut ribbon into 17-inch lengths. Lay ribbon lengths onto fusible webbing strips. Press, following manufacturer's instructions.

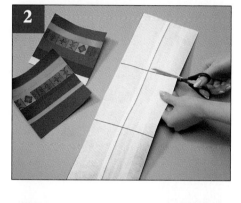

2. Cut ribbon-fused strips into as many 5⅝-inch squares as possible.

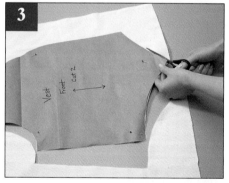

3. From muslin, cut both halfs of front of vest.

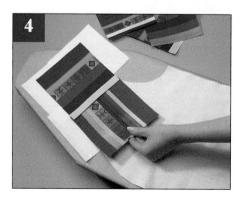

4. Remove paper backing from ribbon squares. Arrange ribbon squares on one half of vest-front, overlapping cut ribbon edges with finished ribbon edges. Completely cover this half of muslin vest-front. Before pressing in place, slide paper backing (shiny side up) under overhanging edges so you won't get adhesive from webbing on iron.

5. After pressing, trim excess ribbon.

6. Repeat Steps 4 and 5 for second half of vest-front. (This step is not pictured.)

7. Sew and finish vest according to pattern directions. (This step is not pictured.)

8. Press any ribbon loosened during turning of vest. Use fabric glue to secure problem areas. Sew buttons on vest where major corners of ribbon squares meet.

Springtime Shadow Appliqué

INTERMEDIATE

Many wearable-art projects emphasize primary colors, but this delicate design features the soft pastels of silk flowers.

What You'll Need

White t-shirt

2 bunches of silk flowers in two sizes and colors (we used large pink mums and small purple violets)

1 bunch of silk ivy leaves

½ yard organza or chiffon

Approximately 100 pearls, 3mm each

15 to 20 crystal E beads

4 acrylic stars, 15mm each

2 yards lace with bound edge, ½ inch wide

Tissue paper, or clear self-adhesive shelving paper

Fusible webbing

2 pressing cloths

Measuring tape

Pencil

Scissors

Shirt board

Fabric glue

Straight pins

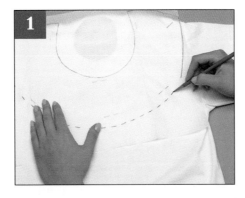

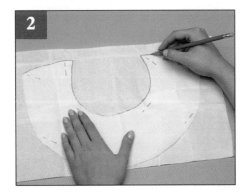

1. Lay t-shirt on flat surface. Pull shoulder seams slightly forward so they are visible at front of shirt. Smooth the rest of shirt out into its true shape. Cut a piece of tissue paper or clear shelving paper large enough to cover front of t-shirt from approximately armhole to armhole and from about top of shoulder to below armholes. Lay tissue paper over top of shirt and pin in place. If using clear shelving paper, remove paper backing and adhere sticky side to top of shirt. Determine top of yoke pattern by tracing around neckline about one inch below neck ribbing. Measure shoulder seam to determine width of yoke pattern. The length of the shoulder seam is the width of the yoke pattern. Measure and mark that distance in regular increments as you move measuring tape around the neck (where you have marked off the top of the yoke pattern). Complete pattern by tracing shoulder seams. See photo for clarity. If using tissue paper, mark an "X" on right side of the pattern.

2. Remove tissue or shelving paper pattern from shirt and cut out yoke along outline. Pin pattern wrong side up on paper backing of fusible webbing and trace yoke pattern. If using shelving paper, remove paper backing and stick pattern to adhesive side of web; then trace. Remove pattern and cut yoke out of adhesive web along outline.

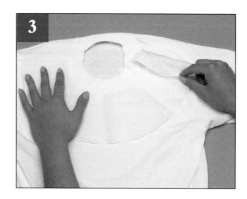

3. Place fusible webbing, adhesive side down, on t-shirt. Adjust and smooth out t-shirt so webbing covers entire yoke area below neck ribbing. Following manufacturer's instructions, bond web to t-shirt. Remove paper backing.

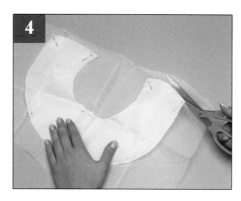

4. Pin or stick pattern right side up on organza and cut yoke out. Leave pattern attached to organza yoke until you are ready to use it to identify the right side of the yoke. Set aside.

5. Remove silk flowers and leaves from stems. Separate layers of flowers. Some flowers may require wire cutters to remove center. Discard any plastic parts of flowers, including centers. Press flowers and leaves to flatten, slightly. Arrange flowers and leaves over webbing, overlapping as desired. When satisfied with arrangement, "tack" in place by pressing the point of a hot iron to each flower and leaf for one or two seconds.

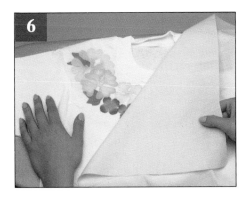

6. Remove yoke pattern from organza yoke and place organza yoke right side up over floral arrangement, covering all of the webbing. Cover yoke area with pressing cloth. Following manufacturer's instructions, bond floral arrangment under organza to t-shirt. Pressing cloth may stick to organza slightly but can be removed with a gentle pull.

7. Slip t-shirt over shirt board. Working on one flower at a time, squeeze a small circle of fabric glue on center of a larger flower. Drop about 15 to 20 pearls into glue, using a toothpick to roll them into place. The size of glue circle and number of pearls needed will vary with each flower. On smallest flowers, place a drop of glue in center of each and place 3 crystal E beads in glue. Arrange acrylic stars on t-shirt. Carefully lifting each star from shirt, use toothpick to coat back of stars with fabric glue. Glue stars back in place on garment. Allow glue to dry.

8. Cut a piece of lace long enough to fit along bottom edge of yoke from shoulder to shoulder. Starting at right shoulder, squeeze a 3-inch line of glue along bottom edge of organza. With ruffles pointing down, press bound edge of lace into glue. Pin in place every inch, inserting pin through lace, t-shirt, and into shirt board. Repeat gluing procedure along entire bottom of yoke. Trim away excess lace. Cut a piece of lace long enough to fit along top edge of yoke and repeat this step, gluing lace to shirt just below neck ribbing. Cut 2 pieces of lace to fit over each shoulder seam. Glue to shirt at each shoulder.

Dress up the
HOLIDAYS

Christmas holly and Halloween ghosts, winter snowflakes and summer fireworks. From spooky suspenders to poinsettia cardigans, wearables can brighten up any holiday. Holidays and festive affairs are the ideal opportunities not only to craft wearables but also to show them off. The pageantry and traditions of Christmas, the costumes and atmosphere of Halloween, and the colors and sparkle of Independence Day provide enough motifs and patterns to decorate wearables for the whole family. "Sparkling Lights" and "Patched Vest and Hat" are Christmas ensembles that both teenagers and adults will find perfect for family celebrations. "Halloween Socks" and "Stars and Stripes" prove that Christmas isn't the only holiday that brings out the crafter in everyone. Any one of these projects will surely dress up your holidays.

Embellished Holiday Vest

INTERMEDIATE

Looking for something to add panache to your wardrobe? Nothing says elegance like this lacy vest. It's the perfect companion for a silky blouse.

What You'll Need

Vest

Assorted lace, doilies, and trims

Holly-print fabric

Lightweight fusible webbing (enough to cover holly print, lace, and doilies)

Assorted brass charms

Clear fabric paint

Fabric tack glue

Industrial-strength adhesive glue (optional)

Scissors

Straight pins

Needle

Thread to match

Aluminum foil

Iron and ironing board

Shirt board

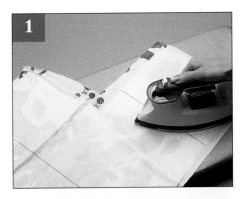

1. Following manufacturer's instructions, iron lightweight fusible webbing to wrong side of holly fabric. Cut out and peel off paper from holly appliqués.

2. Lay vest flat. Move holly appliqués, laces, doilies, and trims into a balanced arrangement that you like before proceeding. Trim pieces to fit vest where needed as shown. You may want to pin pieces in place.

3. Remove one piece at a time to attach webbing. Following manufacturer's instructions, apply lightweight fusible webbing to back side of laces and doilies. It is important to use aluminum foil to protect iron and ironing board from adhesive when applying webbing to lace fabrics and doilies.

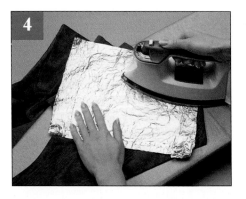

4. Remove paper backing from webbed laces and doilies and attach to vest. Again, use foil on top of these items when ironing them to vest to protect iron. Rub hand over appliqués to make sure edges are secured. Iron again if necessary, though ironing should take no longer than three to seven seconds.

5. Iron holly-fabric appliqués onto vest. Use fabric tack glue to secure heavier edges of doilies to the vest.

6. Put vest on shirt board. Squeeze a fine line of clear fabric paint around edges of holly appliqués to hold in place. Let dry.

7. You may either machine or hand sew charms and trim into place. Charms may also be attached with industrial-strength adhesive glue. Keep adding trims and charms until you are satisfied with the composition.

Sparkling Lights

INTERMEDIATE

Whether you live in the frozen North or the balmy South, your holidays will be brighter with this dazzling set. When you wear our sweater, sock, and shoe ensemble, you'll have it made in the shade!

What You'll Need

White cotton sweater

White socks

White canvas shoes

Soft sparkling fabric paint in gold, sapphire blue, spring green, and dusty rose

Disappearing-ink pen

Black fabric marker with a fine point

Pencil

Flat shader fabric brush with soft bristles

2 yards twine or string

Scissors

White paper

Shirt board

Cardboard tubes

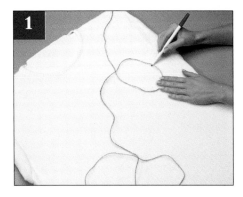

1. Put sweater on shirt board. Drape length of twine from sweater's left shoulder to lower right edge, forming loops as desired. (Be sure to make loops large enough to accommodate lightbulb pattern added in next step.) Leaving twine in place, draw continuous line next to it with disappearing-ink pen.

2. Trace Christmas tree light pattern onto white paper. (Patterns can be found on page 155.) Cut out. Starting at shoulder, place socket of lightbulb on line and draw around pattern onto sweater with disappearing-ink pen. Move pattern to opposite side of line, about 2½ inches down twine line. Trace on sweater. Repeat for entire length of line.

3. Draw over all lines with black fabric marker, omitting any lines that go through already-drawn lightbulbs, as shown. Following manufacturer's instructions, wash out the visible disappearing-ink lines before painting.

Any kind of soft fabric paint can be used to make this sweater ensemble. For different looks, try different paints. Paint formulated for use on dark fabrics will yield a brighter sweater. For a light look without the sparkles, use brush-on fabric paints designed for use with shaded transfers.

4. Paint all lightbulb sockets with gold paint. Paint lightbulbs with the three remaining colors, repeating alternating color pattern as you go down the sweater.

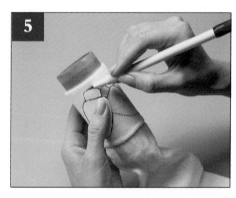

5. For socks, fold down cuff as shown. One at a time, insert cardboard tube into ankle portion of sock. (This will prevent paint from bleeding through to other side.) Draw on lightbulb pattern with disappearing-ink pen on outer ankle of sock, using photo as a guide. Move pattern so it overlaps and draw second bulb with lines stopping at edge of first bulb. Draw over lines with black fabric marker. Paint with alternating pattern as on sweater.

6. For shoes, use the disappearing-ink pen to draw around lightbulb pattern, putting one bulb on the toe, heel, and each side. Work your way around shoe with pattern, overlapping bulbs but not the previously drawn lines. Trace over lines with black fabric marker. Paint with alternating pattern as on sweater, or as desired.

Halloween Socks

INTERMEDIATE

This embellished footwear can be the finishing touch for a costume or provide a subtle way to share your Halloween spirit. Treat your feet to something special.

What You'll Need

Black socks

Flat organza ribbon, 1⅜ inches wide (enough to go around the stretched edges of the sock ribbing)

Brass charms

Sewing machine

Needle

Black thread

1. Lay one sock at a time flat on work area. Do not fold cuff on sock. Stretch the ribbing of the sock as shown.

2. Position the flat ribbon so approximately ¾ inch is over ribbing. Remainder of ribbon should extend off top of sock. This is how a double ruffle effect is achieved. With a sewing machine, straight stitch through ribbon along the very outer edge of ribbing, making sure to keep ribbing fully stretched while stitching. The ribbon will look ruffled when ribbing is returned to shape. Repeat Steps 1 and 2 on second sock.

3. Turn down ribbing to form a cuff on both socks. Hand stitch charms on turned-down cuff so they will show on ankles when worn.

Lacy Angel Christmas Vest

INTERMEDIATE

A vest magically becomes a holiday fashion statement—frosted with lace trim and a winsome angel, accented with stars and sparkling jewels. All this was made with an iron and paint. Not a stitch was taken!

What You'll Need

Vest

1 yard fusible webbing

½ yard scalloped border lace, with star motif

Iron

Wax paper

12 × 6-inch piece of white washable satin

Several 3 × 6-inch pieces of muslin

Brown fabric marker

15mm ombre metallic thread

Fabric paint in ivory, gold, and glitter

20 crystal acrylic rhinestone, 7mm and 8mm

Fabric glue

Iron

1. Lay wrong side of lace on fusible webbing and cover other side with wax paper. Place iron on medium setting and press for three to five seconds. Flip over and iron on paper side of webbing and press for another three seconds. Pull wax paper off lace while still warm. Let cool. Pull lace off webbing paper and cut into desired shapes (extra adhesive will stick to lace in sheet form, trim when cutting shapes; adhesive in the holes will melt into fabric). Leave four stars uncut for angel wings.

2. Iron webbing to back of satin and muslin. Place iron on medium setting on paper side of webbing, press for three to five seconds. Trace patterns on the paper back of prepared materials. Use white for two angel dresses and muslin for two head circles. Cut out and peel paper off appliqué pieces.

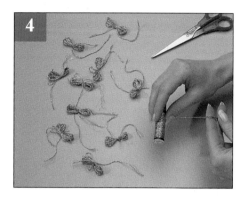

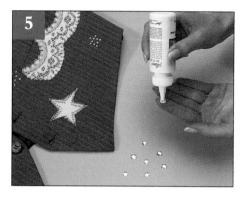

3. Place scalloped border around neckline of vest and top of left pocket. Assemble angels, one on right side of vest and one on back. Position extra lace stars around vest. Iron to adhere pieces.

4. With marker, draw face on head following pattern. (Pattern can be found on page 155.) Make 14 loopy pompoms by winding metallic thread around two fingers 12 times, tie off in center using a separate piece of thread. Glue seven pom-poms around angel head using fabric glue. Repeat for other angel.

5. Outline lace and stars with gold fabric paint and angel with ivory fabric paint (rest tip on edge to steady line). Add ivory dots to make extra fill-in stars. Glue rhinestones to vest with fabric glue.

Halloween Button Covers

INTERMEDIATE

Halloween is a wonderful time of year for crafting. With a few scraps of material, some press and peel foil, and a hot glue gun, you can have fun making these fashionable button covers.

What You'll Need

Scraps of white, black, and orange fabrics

Poster board

Fusible webbing

Press and peel foil kit (kit contains foil, dimensional bond, foil sealer, and applicator brush)

Button covers

Hot glue gun

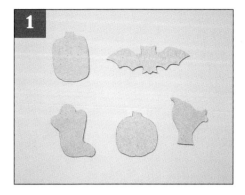

1. Using patterns on page 156, trace shapes onto cardboard and cut. Set aside.

2. Following manufacturer's instructions, iron fusible webbing to fabric. (This step is not pictured.)

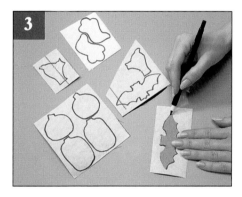

3. Trace a front and back for each cardboard shape onto the fused fabric, then cut out.

4. Fuse fabric shapes onto front and back of cardboard shapes cut out in Step 1. Trim any excess fabric or cardboard from edges. (This step is not pictured.)

5. Following manufacturer's directions in press and peel kit, outline edges of shapes and draw in details using dimensional bond. Let dry until clear. Apply foil by rubbing firmly over dimensional bond with finger. Peel back excess foil from top. Edges and details of shapes should be covered by foil.

Press and peel foil comes in a wide variety of colors. Try making patterns appropriate for other holidays, once you've mastered Halloween. A simple pine tree shape and star would make fine Christmas button covers.

6. Glue button covers to back of each shape using hot glue gun. Press down on button cover to secure firmly.

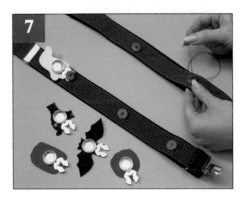

7. Sew buttons to favorite cap, suspenders, shoes, socks, or t-shirts, and fasten button covers to the buttons.

Stars and Stripes

INTERMEDIATE

Be patriotic all summer long in this t-shirt and cap ensemble. The pattern is so quick and simple that you can easily make caps for the whole family and wear them to that Fourth of July picnic.

What You'll Need

White high-necked t-shirt

White cap

⅜ yard waste canvas, # 8½ mesh

Embroidery needle and thread

DMC embroidery floss: 4 skeins yellow, 3 skeins red, 2 skeins blue

Crewel needle

Embroidery hoop

10 white buttons, ½ inch each

1. For cap, cut a 3½ × 8-inch rectangle of waste canvas. With sewing thread, baste waste canvas to center front of cap, about ½ inch above brim. Use full strand of floss to work cross-stitches. Following chart, work each cross-stitch over two spaces of waste canvas, placing needle in tiniest holes of the canvas. (Be careful to stitch within holes, catching the canvas makes pulling out canvas threads difficult.) Keep the tension of stitches taut. When stitching is complete, dampen canvas and remove. Pull vertical threads first, one at a time, then horizontal threads. Let dry. Sew a button to center of each star, using full strand of red floss.

2. For t-shirt, position cross-stitch motifs, placing some single stars among stars with tails. Cut seven 3½ × 8-inch rectangles for complete motifs and six 3 × 3-inch squares for individual stars. Following instructions for cap, work motifs and finish shirt.

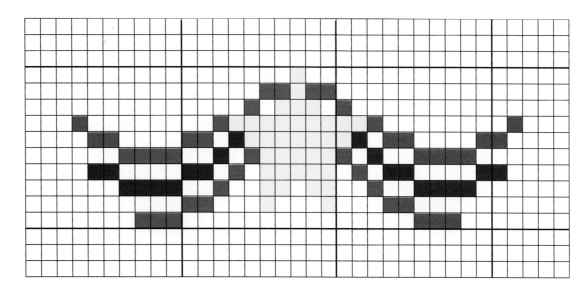

☐ Yellow
■ Red
■ Blue

Cascading Snowflakes

BEGINNER

With fusible webbing, appliqués made from any material are not only possible but easy to do. These lacy, white snowflaké appliqués dress up an ordinary sweatshirt to make a winter wonderland wearable. So, let it snow!

What You'll Need

Sweatshirt

White lace curtain panel, or ½ yard white lace

½ yard fusible webbing

Fabric paint in white slick and diamond

Scissors

Wax paper

Iron and ironing board

Shirt board

1. Trace snowflake patterns (one large, three medium, and five small) on paper side of webbing. (Patterns on page 157.) Lay webbing adhesive-side up on ironing board. Cover with layer of lace, then cover with wax paper, wax-side down. Iron webbing, lace, and wax paper together by placing iron (medium setting) on wax paper; press three to five seconds. Turn over and press on paper side of webbing. Cut out snowflakes as traced.

2. Remove paper and position lace on sweatshirt (use photo for guide). Cover snowflakes with wax paper and iron three to seven seconds (remove paper while still warm). Rub hand over appliqués, checking bond on all edges. If necessary, repeat ironing with wax paper in place to better secure appliqués.

3. Put sweatshirt on shirt board. To paint details, rest tip of fabric paint bottle on appliqué/shirt edge. We outlined snowflakes in white slick and varied inside detail in each snowflake. We added filler snowflakes (narrow "X" divided in half horizontally with third line) and dots with diamond. Let dry.

Patched Vest and Hat

INTERMEDIATE

You'll be amazed how easy it is to put together this striking vest and hat ensemble. Fusible webbing and heat expandable stitch paint make this outfit a snap to produce and fun to wear. The heat expandedable stitch paint gives the illusion of a true blanket stitch.

What You'll Need

Black vest

Black hat

Cotton fabric in golden yellow, green, blue, and red, ⅛ yard each

⅔ yard fusible webbing

Heat expandable stitch paint in buttercup, bright green, marina blue, and cherry red

Pencil

Scissors

White paper

Iron and ironing board

Shirt board

1. Cut an 8-inch piece from each length of fabric. Cut four 4½ × 8-inch pieces of fusible webbing. Following manufacturer's instructions, fuse webbing to wrong side of fabric. (This step is not pictured.)

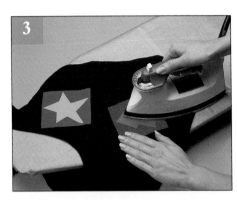

2. You will use some of the fusible webbed fabric for patches and some for the shapes. Keep this in mind when cutting. For patches, cut approximately 3⅝ × 4¼-inch piece from blue fabric; 3 × 3⅞-inch piece from green fabric; one 4 × 4⅛-inch piece and one 2 × 2¼-inch piece from red fabric. Trace patterns for star, bell, large tree, and small tree on white paper. (Patterns can be found on page 158.) Cut out patterns. Use the remaining fusible webbed fabric for the shapes. Place cutout paper patterns for star and bell on yellow fabric and trace. Trace large and small tree patterns on green fabric. Cut out all traced shapes.

3. Put vest on ironing board. Place yellow star on blue patch, green trees on red patches, and yellow bell on green patch. Lay patches on vest and hat for placement. One patch at a time, remove paper backing from both pieces and replace on vest. Use iron to fuse both at same time according to manufacturer's instructions. Using the small red patch and small green tree, repeat for hat.

4. Put vest on shirt board. Duplicate a blanket stitch with stitching paint. Touch tip of paint bottle to outside edge of each appliqué (touching both vest and patch or patch and shape) and make a series of small sideways "L" shapes with "L" extending onto appliqué. Use photo as a guide. We outlined the yellow star in green, the blue patch in red, the green tree in buttercup, the red patch in blue, the yellow bell in blue, and the green patch in red. Complete one patch at a time, turning shirt board so that the edge you are working on is always at the top. Repeat for hat patch, matching colors with vest patch.

5. After vest and hat have dried for 12 hours, expand paint following manufacturer's instructions.

Folk Art Christmas Tree

Let the games begin! You're sure to be a hit in this embellished cardigan. The festive colors you paint on this design add a splash of fun that really perks up your party clothes.

What You'll Need

White cotton knit cardigan

Buttons to coordinate with design, same number and size as on existing cardigan

Soft fabric paints in dark green, golden yellow, red, and black

Black iron-on transfer pen

Black fabric paint marker, fine point

Medium round fabric paint brush, soft bristles

Straight pins

Needle

White thread

White paper

Iron and ironing board

Shirt board

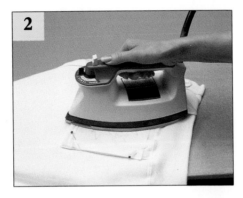

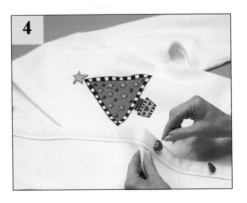

1. You will need a total of three patterns for this project. Using iron-on transfer pen, trace tree pattern onto white paper, placing star on top of tree. (Pattern on page 159.) This is for the back of cardigan. To make pattern fit crest area, reduce on photo copier at 78 percent. Trace crest pattern on cardigan. Cut a piece of paper the size of pocket. Place over stars on tree pattern. With transfer pen, trace a cluster of stars, both large and small. This is the pattern for the pocket.

2. Center large traced tree pattern face down on back of cardigan. Pin in place. Use iron to transfer pattern to cardigan, following manufacturer's instructions on transfer pen. Turn cardigan over and position small tree pattern face down on left side. Transfer as before. Repeat with star cluster on right pocket as shown.

3. Place on shirt board with back of cardigan face up. Paint design using finished photograph as a guide. Be sure you allow drying time in between colors to avoid smearing. Apply second coat to any color if necessary. To complete the look, trace over all transfer lines with black fabric paint marker. Repeat paint procedure on front of cardigan, painting both tree and stars.

4. When shirt is completely dry, follow manufacturer's instructions to heat-set paint. Remove buttons from cardigan and replace with your chosen buttons to finish. We used heart-shaped buttons to accent the design on the tree.

Poinsettia Cardigan

ADVANCED

No one will ever know that this holiday cardigan was a sweatshirt. Use fabric paint and some household staples to create the beginnings of a wonderful holiday outfit. Wear this over slacks and a blouse and the Christmas tree will not be the only thing that shines in your house.

What You'll Need

Black sweatshirt, one size larger than you normally wear

Fabric paint in white, red, and dark green

Soft metallic paint in platinum

Glitter dimensional fabric paint in champagne

Pearl dimensional fabric paint in ruby red pearl

Slick dimensional fabric paint in green

Brown paper or newspaper

9 × 15-inch piece of tulle netting

Masking tape

Fine point marker

White fabric pencil

½-inch flat brush

Small water container for rinsing brushes

Wax paper

Household sponge, cut in holly leaf shape

Ruler

Pinking shears

Washable fabric glue

Iron

Shirt Board

1. Photocopy the pattern from page 160 and enlarge 112 percent. Cover work surface with brown paper or newspaper. Tape the tulle netting on top of the paper and on the work surface to secure. Trace poinsettia pattern with fine point permanent marker.

2. Put sweatshirt on shirt board. Use a white pencil to draw a straight line down the center of the shirt. Transfer the poinsettia patterns through the tulle to the shirt using the white pencil. (Patterns are on page 160.) Be sure to watch the placement of the poinsettia flowers, keeping them at least one inch away from the center line.

3. Using the edge of a dry paintbrush, brush red fabric paint along the top edge of the petals. Immediately begin to pull some of the paint into the center of the petal using the flat side of the brush. Do not fill in the entire petal with paint. The black shirt will show through the thinner areas of paint.

4. Add additional paint in some areas to create highlights. Run a thin line of paint along the lower edge of the petal to define the bottom shape. Repeat for the other petals. Make some poinsettias red and others white. Remember to work with a dry brush, using water only to rinse out a color after you are finished with it.

5. Pour a small amount of dark green fabric paint on a piece of wax paper. Cover one side of the dry holly leaf-shaped sponge lightly with paint. Lightly sponge several holly leaves between the poinsettias.

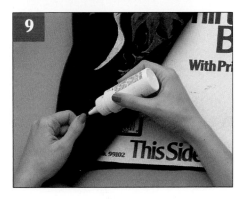

6. Using the white pencil, draw in a ribbon. Fill in the area with the platinum soft metallic paint.

7. If desired, squeeze on a few thin accent lines to several poinsettia petals using the champagne glitter dimensional paint. Immediately brush out the paint into the petal. This will add a shimmer to a few petals (we did this on the white poinsettias). Add dots of champagne glitter to the center of each poinsettia.

8. Add a few beads of ruby red paint for holly berries between the leaves and flowers. Outline and add veins to each holly leaf using the slick green dimensional paint. Do not make a solid line. Add a few tendrils between the leaves and flowers, if desired.

9. Let the sweatshirt dry flat overnight. Using pinking shears, cut down the center line of the sweatshirt front. Fold under approximately ½ inch on each side and iron the edge of the back side. Run a line of washable fabric glue under the edge and push down on the material to adhere. Let dry thoroughly. Heat-set dark green, red, and white fabric paint with a dry iron set to a temperature to match the sweatshirt fabric.

Candy Canes and Snowflakes

BEGINNER

Here are some peppermint candy canes that even your dentist won't mind you having around. This appliquéd shirt is enhanced by sprinkling glitter on the painted snowflakes.

What You'll Need

Sweatshirt

Appliqué material (we used Diamond Dust Panel 7515-R)

1 yard fusible webbing, 17 inches wide

Fabric paints in gold glitter and white opal

Clear prismatic glitter

Scissors

Wax paper

Iron and ironing board

Shirt board

1. Cut out appliqué areas needed from yardage or panel. Do not cut out in detail; leave ½-inch border around fabric pattern you intend to use. Place fabric cutouts on adhesive side of fusible webbing, facing right side up. Cover with wax paper. Iron (medium setting) on wax paper, pressing for three to five seconds. Turn over and press another three to five seconds. Pull wax paper off while still warm. Cut out appliqués in detail. Peel off paper backing.

2. Position appliqués around neckline, then iron in place. Rub hand over appliqués to make sure all edges are secured. If necessary, touch up edges with iron, but use caution not to heat excessively. Ironing should take only three to seven seconds maximum.

3. Put shirt on shirt board. Rest tip of fabric paint bottle on edge of appliqué/sweatshirt and outline each piece. Accent detail on appliqués with matching color or clear prismatic fabric glitter. We used gold glitter fabric paint to highlight the pinecones and bells. We also outlined the bows, candy canes, holly, and berries with white opal fabric paint. Let dry.

4. Add painted snowflakes for fillers using white opal fabric paint. Snowflake placement may vary, according to personal taste. Make a narrow "X" and add a horizontal third line to divide the "X" in half. Now you will have a six-point basic snowflake; add circles, dots, or lines to modify each flake. Add more variety by changing sizes from largest (3-inch diameter), to medium (1½-inch diameter, still embellished), to small (¾-inch diameter, not embellished). Add dots of paint to fill. Sprinkle lightly with clear prismatic fabric glitter while paint is still wet. Let dry. Shake off excess glitter.

Fun to Make,
FUN TO WEAR

Charms and glitter, tie-dye and lace doilies. From baggy boxers to funky shoe frills, these whimsical projects are as much fun to make as they are to wear. Aside from being economical and creative, one of the charming aspects about crafting wearables is the sheer fun of it all. The projects in this chapter guarantee good times and a chuckle here and there. If you're looking for an adorable wearable for your little boy, which is not an easy task considering most wearables are for girls, then he'll love "Planes, Trains, and Automobiles." "Lacy T with Boxers" and "Happy Feet" prove that you can embellish just about any article of clothing, while "Embellished Jacket" offers a more refined design that is nonetheless fun to craft. Rummage through this section if you're looking for a project made from unusual materials, a design created for an uncommon article of clothing, or a wearable that is fun to fabricate.

Making a Splash!

If your son or daughter excels at a particular sport, this wearable is a great way to display their team spirit. With this project, you can transfer the team's best photo to your child's favorite t-shirt so they can show off their winning team with pride.

What You'll Need

White t-shirt

Color photocopy of photograph. (If there are numbers or letters, use a mirror-image copy.)

Photo transfer medium

Blue sparkling dimensional fabric paint

Soft sparkling fabric paint in blue

Fabric paint brushes (we used a flat shader and a medium round)

1-inch sponge brush

Wax paper

Rolling pin

Iron and ironing board

Pressing cloth

Washable fabric glue

White paper for tracing patterns

Black marker

Disappearing-ink pen

Shirt board

1. Place shirt on shirt board. If your shirt board has dried paint on it, cover it with wax paper, because dried paint may transfer to the inside of your shirt and discolor your photo. Trim all white edges from photocopy. Lay photocopy face up on waxed paper. Apply a thick layer of transfer medium with finger or sponge brush. Be sure all edges and corners have been covered.

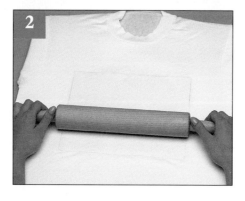

2. Place photocopy face down on center of shirt, about 3½ inches from base of neckline. Smooth onto shirt with rolling pin, making sure to remove any air bubbles. If any transfer medium is pressed out of the sides, wipe it up immediately. Dry flat for 24 hours.

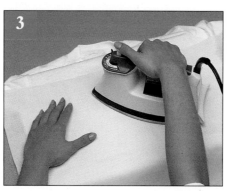

3. After 24 hours, remove shirt from shirt board and heat set both sides of transfer for 30 seconds using a pressing cloth and a dry iron on a wool setting. Let cool.

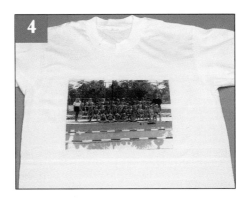

4. Soak shirt in water for 30 to 60 minutes. Squeeze water from shirt but do not wring transfer area. Lay shirt on a flat surface. Using fingers, gently rub paper backing. Work from the center to the outside edges. When you have removed the first layer of paper, soak shirt for another 15 minutes. Remove from water, repeating process until all paper particles have been removed. Be careful when rubbing edges so as not to tear the transfer. Let shirt dry flat.

TIP

The splash design works well with a swimming picture and blue paint, but you can also use the same pattern with any team photo for any sport. Simply change the paint to the colors of your team or other colors that will coordinate with your photo, and you can make a splash even if you're not a swimmer!

5. When all paper particles have been removed and shirt is dry, return shirt to shirt board. Pour a puddle of washable glue onto palette and use sponge brush to apply a thin coat to the transfer area. Set aside to dry.

6. Trace splash patterns onto separate sheets of white paper with black marker. (Patterns are on page 161 of this book.) Place patterns inside shirt above and to right of transfer, aligning corners of splash with corner of photo. Trace patterns onto shirt with disappearing-ink pen. Repeat, moving patterns below and to left of transfer.

7. Use fabric paint brushes to brush soft sparkling fabric paint inside of splash lines. Squeeze sparkling blue dimensional paint from bottle in a line around the edge of the transfer. Use the flat shader brush to flatten line of paint in a wavy fashion.

Sunflowers

BEGINNER

Big, bold, and beautiful, sunflowers make a colorful fashion statement in any season. You can add a touch of sunshine to any t-shirt with these simple appliqués and a little fabric paint.

What You'll Need

Long-sleeved t-shirt with scoop neck (we used off-white poly/cotton)

Pair of slouch socks (we used off white)

Sunflower pattern fabric

Fabric paint in green, brown, and gold

Disappearing-ink pen

Fabric glue

Ruler

Craft stick or small paint brush

Scissors

Shirt board

Wax paper

Craft paper to cover work surface

1. Cut out five sunflowers from fabric. Four of these should be medium-sized sunflowers with one leaf each, and one should be a large sunflower with a portion of a leaf. Set aside two of the medium-sized flowers for socks.

2. Slide shirt onto shirt board and lay flat on work surface. Measure and mark positioning of sunflowers on shirt with disappearing-ink pen and ruler. Measure and mark 3 to 5 inches below each shoulder and mark center front approximately 1 inch below collar. Sunflowers should be about 2 inches apart after placement.

3. Place sunflower cutouts upside down on craft paper. Squeeze thin layer of fabric glue onto back side of cutout and spread with craft stick. Glue sunflowers on shirt at markings. Place large sunflower in center and the two smaller sunflowers under shoulders. Point leaf on left side facing bottom of shirt and the leaf on the right side facing top of shirt. Press around edges of cutouts to make sure edges are glued down. Add extra glue if needed. Let dry 24 hours.

4. Outline sunflowers with fabric paints. Gently squeeze a thin line of gold paint around outside edges of petals and green around leaves. Squeeze dots of green and brown paint in center of sunflower. Let paint dry 24 hours.

5. Slide piece of wax paper inside of socks and lay flat on work surface. Measure and mark positioning of sunflower on each sock with disappearing marker and ruler. Measure and mark 1 inch below top of each sock.

TIP

With the socks, make sure that appliqués are on one side of right sock and opposite side of left sock. When the socks are on your feet, the sunflowers should be on the outside of both ankles.

6. Place sunflower cutout upside down on craft paper. Squeeze thin layer of fabric glue onto back side of cutout and spread with craft stick or small paint brush. Glue sunflower on socks at markings. Press around edges of cutouts with fingers to make sure all edges are glued down. Add extra glue if needed. Let glue dry 24 hours.

7. Outline sunflower with fabric paints. Gently squeeze a thin line of gold paint around outside edges of petals and green around leaves. Squeeze dots of green and brown paint in center of sunflower. Let paint dry 24 hours.

Go West

Whether line dancing at your local watering hole or whooping it up with the boys, western wear is all the rage. Turn a plain white shirt into a Wild West wearable with just a few appliqués.

What You'll Need

Long-sleeved button down shirt (we used white)

Western print fabric

Fabric webbing spray (we used teal and gold)

Black fabric paint

Jewelry gems (we used stars and circles)

Scissors

Fabric glue

Shirt board

Ruler

Disappearing-ink pen

Craft stick or small paint brush

Craft paper to cover work surface

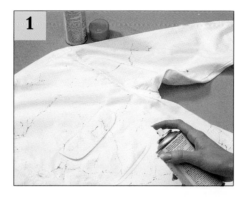

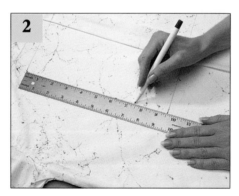

1. Place shirt on shirt board and lay flat on work surface covered with craft paper. Spray shirt with webbing spray. Shake can and hold about 12 inches away from shirt. Spray quickly across shirt. Repeat with second color. Let shirt dry about 15 minutes and then repeat on the back side of the shirt. Sleeves should not be tucked in, because they need to be sprayed with fabric webbing as well.

2. Cut out nine square western motifs from fabric, 3 × 3 inches. Also cut out one hat, one pair of boots, and two diamond-shaped motifs. Measure and mark back side of shirt with ruler and disappearing-ink pen. Mark a square 9½ × 9½ inches in center back of shirt.

3. Place motifs upside down on craft paper. Squeeze fabric glue on back side and spread with craft stick or small paint brush. Glue the nine square motifs onto back of shirt, starting with top left corner. Align with markings. Glue along markings approximately ¼ inch apart. Press in place with finger. Let dry 20 minutes to allow glue to bond.

4. Turn shirt over and glue cowboy hat to upper left corner, glue cowboy boots to right pocket and diamond shapes to front of sleeve cuffs. Press in place with fingers to make sure all edges are glued securely. Allow entire shirt to dry 24 hours.

5. Outline motifs with black fabric paint. Gently squeeze a thin line of black paint around outside edges. Highlight some details inside motifs if desired.

6. Glue gems with fabric glue. Allow shirt to dry 24 hours.

Lacy T with Boxers

BEGINNER

Lounge around the house in this comfy cotton t-shirt with matching boxers. The white cotton lace adds a personal, feminine touch.

What You'll Need

- T-shirt

- Cotton boxer shorts

- Two 5-inch square lace motifs

- Two 3-inch round lace motifs

- One 2½-inch round lace motif

- Disappearing-ink pen

- Ruler

- Fabric glue

- Craft stick or small paint brush

- Shirt board

- Wax paper

- Scissors

- Craft paper to cover work surface

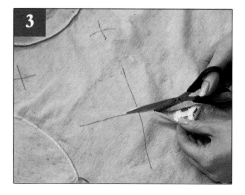

1. Lay t-shirt flat on work surface and insert shirt board. Measure and mark with disappearing-ink pen. The 3-inch round motifs should be placed about 2 to 5 inches from shoulder seam and 2 inches from start of sleeve seam to edge of lace. The 2½-inch motif should be centered between the two shoulder motifs and placed one to 3 inches from bottom of collar. Shoulder and center motifs should be approximately 3½ inches apart. For pocket motif, measure and mark 8 inches from top shoulder seam to pocket area to fit 5-inch square motif. Mark approximately 3½ inches from side seam.

2. Turn lace motifs upside down on wax paper. Squeeze fabric glue along edges only. Spread glue with craft stick or small paint brush. Position lace motifs along markings on t-shirt. Press along edges with fingers to make sure all edges are secure. Add more glue if needed. Let dry 24 hours.

3. Remove t-shirt from shirt board and turn inside out. Mark an "X" inside lace motifs with disappearing fabric marker. Cut along "X" with scissors. Trim away the t-shirt behind the lace. Cut along the glued edge as close as possible. Be careful NOT to cut through the lace motif.

4. Lay boxer shorts flat on work surface and insert wax paper into right leg of shorts to ensure that glue does not leak to back side. Measure and mark with disappearing fabric marker 1 inch from bottom right edge.

5. Turn 5-inch square lace motif upside down on wax paper. Squeeze fabric glue along edges only. Spread glue with craft stick or small paint brush. Position lace motif along markings on boxer shorts. Press along edges with fingers to make sure all edges are secure. Add more glue if needed. Let dry 24 hours.

6. Turn boxer shorts inside out and mark an "X" inside lace motif with disappearing marker. Cut along "X" with scissors. Trim away the boxer shorts behind the lace. Cut along the glued edges as closely as possible. Be careful not to cut through the lace motif.

Lunch Tote

INTERMEDIATE

Conservation and the environment are on everyone's mind. Instead of using paper bags to carry your lunch to work or school and then tossing them away, use this reusable canvas lunch tote.

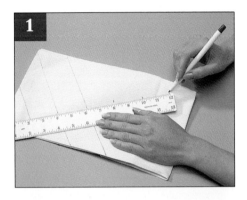

1. Starting from top left corner of lunch tote and moving to bottom right corner, mark a diagonal line across bag every two inches. Use a disappearing-ink pen. You should end up with seven sections.

What You'll Need

Lunch tote bag

Green, purple, garnet red, yellow, and black fabric paints

Disappearing-ink pen

Ruler

2. Draw geometric shapes, lines, squiggles, and dots to create a unique pattern in each section. See finished photo on page 82 for our designs.

3. Trace over markings with fabric paints. Gently squeeze a thin line of fabric paint along all lines. For dots, keep bottle upright and gently squeeze until a dot of paint comes out, then lift off fabric. See finished photo on page 82 for our color suggestions.

Tie-Dye Bouquet

INTERMEDIATE

The secret to a more polished look with tie-dying is to exert more control over the dying process. By updating and refining, this technique will never go out of style.

What You'll Need

White tunic-styled t-shirt and white cotton leggings

Brush-top fabric paint in 4 colors (we used yellow, raspberry, blue, and purple)

Fine point permanent marker in black

Rubber bands

Wax paper

Paper towels

Water in trigger-style sprayer

Blow dryer

Iron and ironing board

1. To begin tie-dye process, put one hand inside neck of shirt and poke up a portion of shirt about 3 inches below neckline. Tightly wrap a rubber band around poked-up section so that about ¾ inch of shirt is gathered above the band.

2. Repeat same procedure on both sides of rubber-banded section, about 3 inches to the outside and slightly below this first section. Do two more about 3 inches lower and about an inch to each side of center. Insert wax paper inside of shirt. Be sure it covers entire area to be painted.

3. Work near an electrical outlet. Have blow dryer and spray bottle filled with water nearby. Open all bottles of paint. Squeeze bottle of yellow paint slightly to get paint flowing and then brush onto paper towel. (In general, do not squeeze bottle while brushing on shirt as you may get a bigger burst of paint than you need. Always move bottle of paint over to paper towels when squeezing more paint onto brush.) Brush yellow paint on all poked up sections of shirt above rubber bands. These will be your flower centers.

4. Brush on other colors below rubber-banded sections in a circle about 1 inch wide. Refer to photo of finished project for recommended color placement.

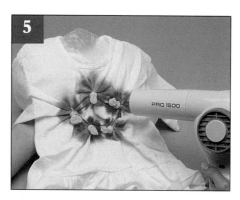

5. Immediately spray a fine mist of water over painted areas. Check folds near rubber bands to make sure that all areas are bleeding. Add more paint or more water, if necessary. Check progress of bleeding often. Stop bleeding by blowing hot air on paint with a blow dryer until nearly dry and paint is no longer bleeding.

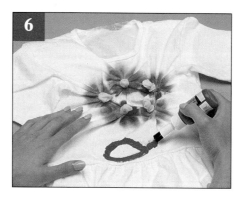

6. Lay shirt flat on work surface, check-ing to make sure wax paper covers entire inside of shirt. Add more wax paper if necessary. Using raspberry paint, make a bow shape below the tie-dye flowers. You may want to remove the rubber bands before painting bow. (You may feel more comfortable practicing the bow on paper towels or an old shirt first.) Mist with water, allow paint to bleed, and then stop bleeding with blow dryer as before. Set shirt aside until completely dry.

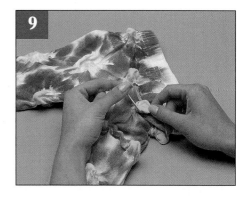

7. When dry, press shirt on the inside with a warm iron to smooth out wrinkles. Replace wax paper. Use black fabric marker to lightly sketch in flower stem, flower petals, and details of bow. (Again, you may want to practice this on an old t-shirt first. Use light, quick strokes for best results.)

8. For leggings, gather sections and tie off with rubber bands, as with shirt. This time, however, use an overall pattern. There should be a poked-up section every few inches. Insert wax paper inside legs and seat of leggings. Paint front of legs first. Use brush top paints as on shirt, coloring centers yellow and selecting flower colors in a random pattern. Try not to put several flowers of the same color next to each other. Immediately mist painted areas with water. Allow to bleed, checking folds as in Step 5 to determine if more paint or water needs to be added. Stop bleeding with blow dryer. Turn leggings over, paint backs of legs, then mist, bleed, and dry as before.

9. Remove all rubber bands from leggings. Keep wax paper inside and set aside until paint is thoroughly dry.

Planes, Trains, and Automobiles

BEGINNER

Your little copilot can pretend to fly high in the sky in this charming sweatshirt, suitable for a boy or girl. With the advantages of fusible webbing, this project is simple to make, even for those beginning crafters.

What You'll Need

Sweatshirt

Scraps of fabric (we used a striped print, red cotton, white cotton, gold lamé, and silver lamé)

Dimensional fabric paints in red, sparkle green, glitter gold, sparkle purple, and pearl white

Fusible webbing

Pencil

Iron and ironing board

Scissors

2 pressing cloths

Shirt board

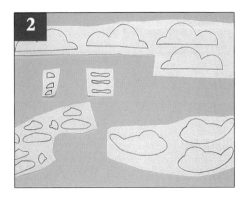

1. Trace pattern pieces for three planes and four clouds onto paper side of fusible webbing, grouping together pieces to be cut from same color fabric. (Pattern can be found on page 162). Note that in the photo to the left, the three plane bodies are grouped together because they will be cut from the striped material, the three noses and six wings are together because they will be cut from the gold lamé, the three propellers will be cut from the red material, the three plane windows will be cut from the silver lamé, and the four clouds will be cut from the white cotton. (Note: If you trace plane pieces so they point to your left, they will point to your right on the finished sweatshirt.)

2. Cut apart pieces in the groupings described in Step 1. Note that in the photo to the left, the three plane bodies have been cut apart as one piece of fusible webbing, the clouds have been cut apart as one piece, and so forth.

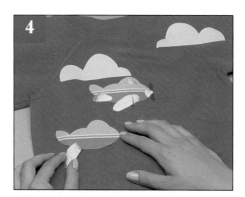

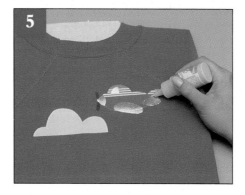

3. Cut fabrics into pieces slightly larger than their corresponding webbing groups. Lay a pressing cloth over ironing board. Lay fabrics wrong side up on pressing cloth. With webbing side against wrong side of fabric, place fusible webbing groups over appropriate pieces of fabric (plane bodies piece over striped fabric, noses and wings piece over gold lamé, etc). Be sure adhesive web does not extend beyond edges of fabric. Cover fusible webbing with second pressing cloth. Following manufacturer's instructions, bond plane pieces to back of fabrics.

4. Cut out each plane piece along outside lines. Remove paper from back from each piece. Arrange clouds and body of planes on front of shirt as desired. Tack these pieces in place by pressing point of a hot iron to each for a second or two. Arrange propeller, window, wings, and nose on body of plane and tack in place. Cover arrangement with second pressing cloth. Following manufacturer's instructions, bond fabric pieces to sweatshirt. Repeat this step, bonding remaining cloud and plane to back of shirt.

5. Slip sweatshirt over shirt board, placing side of shirt to be painted over waxed side of board. Squeezing paints directly from bottle, outline each piece of fabric with fabric paint in color to match. When one side has dried, turn shirt around on board and outline plane and cloud on other side. (Back of shirt shown at left.)

Embellished Jacket

INTERMEDIATE

Thrift stores often yield great bargains in terms of clothing you can embellish for that personal touch. Pick up a men's suit jacket and decorate it with charms, ribbons, and lace.

What You'll Need

Men's jacket

2 large lace appliqués

10 brass charms, including 8 hearts, 1 key, and 1 connecting charm

6 antique gold buttons

4½ feet wine-colored ribbon, ⅛ inch wide

⅜ yard lace trim

⅜ yard satin rose trim

7 ribbon roses

2 buttons, 1 inch diameter

Washable fabric glue

Jewelry glue

Scissors

Needle

Thread to match

1. Place lace appliqués under lapels of jacket until satisfied with arrangement. For small decorations on lapel, simply trim off a couple of the smaller motifs from the appliqués, as shown.

2. Place small motifs on lapel in pleasing design. Use washable fabric glue to secure all pieces of lace in place. Repeat on other side.

3. Lay out charms and small buttons using photo as guide for placement. Use straight pins to help keep in place.

4. Cut ribbon lengths into one 20-inch piece, two 3-inch pieces, one 6-inch piece, one 8-inch piece, and one 4-inch piece. Thread 20-inch piece of ribbon through wide-eyed needle. Begin above charm on right lapel of jacket and thread ribbon through charm. Then loop in a zigzag fashion under and around key and through each button hole. Sew on three antique buttons with needle and thread. Use jewelry glue to secure large heart and key in place. Glue three ribbon roses inside large heart. Tie 3-inch piece of ribbon onto loop of key. (This step is not pictured, but use photo in Step 5 for placement.)

5. For left lapel, sew connecting charm in place. Thread ribbon through loops on connecting charm in following sequence: 6-inch ribbon first, then 8-inch ribbon, and then 4-inch ribbon. Center each piece of ribbon on charm loop and secure with an overhand knot. Thread ribbon ends through loop of heart directly beneath corresponding loop on connecting charm, as shown. Tie ribbon ends in knot so charm can't be removed. Sew each charm to lapel allowing ribbon to hang freely. Sew remaining antique buttons in place just above connecting charm.

6. Cut two 4-inch lengths of ribbon. Cut enough lace trim and satin rose trim to fit top edge of each pocket. Trim edges very carefully. Use washable fabric glue to secure trim in place on both pockets. Tie a 4-inch length of ribbon and thread through loops on charms for each pocket. Tie a knot to secure ribbon. Sew each charm in place. With jewelry glue, secure ribbon roses in place on both pockets.

Keys to My Heart

Many wearable-art projects feature designs that are primarily realistic renderings of animals, plants, or objects. For a change of pace, try this abstract pattern that exploits color to its best advantage.

What You'll Need

Dark-colored t-shirt

Brass charms in key and heart shapes (other charms can be substituted)

Fabric paint in pink, teal, and purple

Fabric paint brushes (we used a flat shader)

White paper for tracing pattern

Pencil

11 × 9-inch piece of tulle

Black marker

Shirt board

Masking tape

White fabric pencil

Iron and ironing board

Needle and thread to match

1. Lay charms you have chosen onto pattern in book to determine whether or not you need to adjust pattern. (Patterns can be found on page 163.) Charms should be placed in empty spaces between design elements. Trace pattern onto white paper, making changes if necessary. Tape tulle onto traced pattern and mark over lines with black marker.

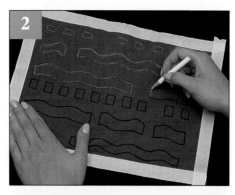

2. Put shirt on shirt board. Position tulle pattern on shirt in desired spot and tape in place. Trace over lines with white fabric pencil. Remove tulle.

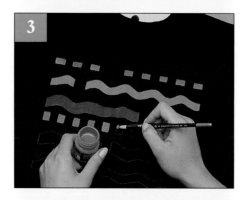

3. To paint, start at top of shirt and work your way down. Rows with rectangles are painted pink, rows with thin waves are teal, and rows with thick waves are purple. On a very dark-colored shirt, you may need to apply a second coat of paint.

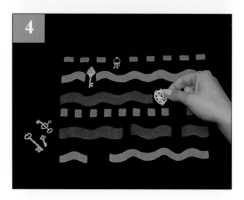

4. When shirt is completely dry, heat-set paint following manufacturer's instructions. Place charms in desired spots and sew.

Happy Feet

BEGINNER

Making your own shoe decorations instead of purchasing more shoes saves money. If you use temporary glue or repositional glue, you can apply different decorations to the same pair of shoes. Save enough to buy a purse and then decorate it to match.

What You'll Need

FOR ALL THREE PROJECTS

Super glue gel

Temporary bond glue (optional)

Scissors

Ruler

Small paint brush

RIBBON AND SUN PENDANT BEADS

⅔ yard flowered ribbon, 1 inch wide

2 vergigris metalessence sun pendant beads, 25 × 7mm each

LACE AND BEADS

⅛ yard scalloped candlelight lace, 1 to 2 inches wide

2 antiquated dark turquoise filigree puff disc beads, 18.5 × 8.5mm each

4 antiquated silver-washed heart beads, 15 × 13.5mm each

Ivory thread

Needle

ROSES, LACE, AND TRIM

6 coral silk ribbon roses, ⅜ inch diameter

⅓ yard pearl ecru lace, ¾ inch wide

⅛ yard scalloped dark mauve trim, 1¾ inch wide

¼ yard dark mauve braid, ¾ inch wide

12 inches floral wire

RIBBON AND SUN PENDANT BEADS

1. Cut two pieces of ribbon at 6 ½ inches each and two pieces at 5 inches each. (This step is not pictured.)

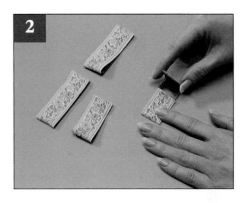

2. With each ribbon, form a loop so that ends of ribbon overlap ½ inch. Flatten out ribbon loops. Glue overlapped ends with super glue gel, as shown. Glue the inside centers of each together.

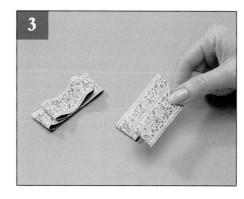

3. Center and glue shorter ribbons onto longer ones.

4. Glue sun pendant bead onto center of each loop.

5. With small brush, apply either temporary glue or super glue gel to shoe decoration, depending on whether you want a permanent hold or not. (We used temporary glue.) Attach to shoes.

LACE AND BEADS

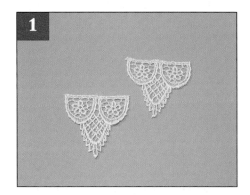

1. Cut two pieces of scalloped candle-light lace, one for each shoe, in configuation shown.

2. With needle and thread, secure beads to lace. Begin by knotting thread to back of lace. Push needle up through lace and run thread through holes in heart bead, then down through lace, and back up again. Repeat with turquoise bead and second heart bead. Secure thread. Repeat for second shoe decoration.

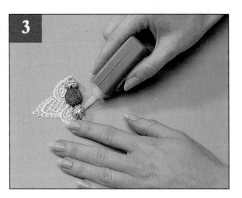

3. A touch of super glue gel, as shown, will secure beads firmly to lace. With temporary or permanent glue, secure decorations to shoes.

ROSES, LACE, AND TRIM

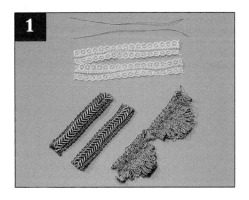

1. Cut two 2⅜-inch pieces from scalloped trim, centering scallop. Cut two 3⅝-inch pieces of braid. Cut two 5-inch pieces of pearl lace. Cut two 6-inch pieces of floral wire.

2. Center and glue braid to top of scalloped trim with super glue gel, alternating braid direction on each trim. Fold edges to back and then glue down.

3. Thread one piece of wire through the top edge of the flower pattern of the lace, as shown. Gather, pulling ends together but leaving a small center hole.

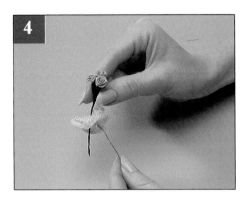

4. Insert three rose stems in the center hole. Pull and twist wire ends together, as shown. Glue roses from bottom side. When dry, cut stems close to lace.

5. Glue rose decorations to center of braids.

6. Glue decorations to shoes with temporary glue, or permanently with super glue gel. (This step is not pictured.)

Decorate
YOUR DENIMS

Y o-yos and gemstones, baubles and beads. From pint-sized overalls for the younger set to jean jackets for your teen, you'll want to decorate denims in these creative ways. Ever since Levi Strauss made the first pair of trousers out of a tough cotton fabric called *serge de Nimes* back in the 1850s, denim has been America's favorite fabric. Durable and sporty, denim is suitable for almost all occasions. A simple design such as "Jumper Jive" uses cloth yo-yos and lace doilies to dress up an ordinary baggy jumper. "Beaded Denim" takes advantage of the array of beads available on the craft market to add character to a shirt and hat ensemble. If you're looking for a challenge, try "Traveler's Jacket," which uses photo-transfer medium to transfer postcards of your favorite vacation spots to that comfortable old jean jacket. Express your individuality by decorating those jeans, jackets, and jumpers.

Jumper Jive

INTERMEDIATE

A plain denim jumper becomes a dressy but comfortable wearable by attaching a bit of lace and a few fabric yo-yos. The latest in embellishments, fabric yo-yos are easy to make and fun to wear.

What You'll Need

Denim jumper

4 coordinating fabrics for flowers, ⅛ yard each

Scraps of 1 or 2 green fabrics for leaves

4 battenburg doilies, each 4 inches in diameter

1 cathedral-shaped doily (optional)

9 small buttons to coordinate with flower fabrics

Needle

Thread to match

Washable fabric glue

Pencil

Scissors

Sewing machine (optional)

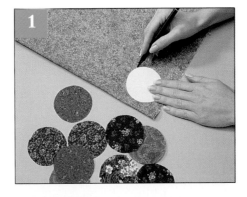

1. Trace a total of nine circles for flower yo-yos onto coordinating fabrics and cut. Trace and cut ten circles from leaf fabrics. (Pattern can be found on page 155.)

2. With needle and thread, use a running stitch and stitch ⅛ inch from top of each flower fabric circle. Sew on wrong side of fabric. As you sew, pull or gather fabric. When completely around circle, pull thread tight and tie thread to secure. Flatten each "ball" to form a fabric yo-yo.

3. Fold each leaf circle in half with right sides of material on outside. Fold the corners into the center and finger press in place.

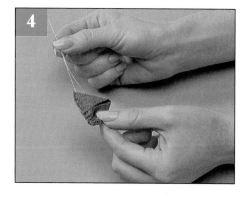

4. With needle and thread, use a running stitch and stitch ⅛ inch from cut edges of leaves. Pull thread tight and secure with knot.

5. Lay jumper flat. Using photo as guide for placement, place battenburg doilies in appropriate positions. With washable fabric glue, secure doilies in place. Glue along all solid edges of doilies to secure bond. (If cathedral doily is to be used as pocket on lower right of jumper, sew in place with machine.)

6. Lay out yo-yo flowers and leaves. Pin and then sew in place using needle and thread. Blind stitch around outside edge of each flower, tucking the leaves underneath the flowers.

7. Sew buttons in center of each flower.

Bo Peep's Sheep

BEGINNER

You'll think that Bo Peep just stepped off the pages of a story book when your little girl steps into these colorful bib overalls.

What You'll Need

Toddler's bib overalls

6 inches pink crinkled ribbon

6 inches yellow crinkled ribbon

9 inches light blue crinkled ribbon

1 yard white crinkled ribbon

18 inches double-faced chartreuse satin ribbon, 1/8 inch wide

Black shank button, 3/8 inch diameter

Scrap of black felt

Scrap of white felt

Large safety pin

Washable fabric glue

Scissors

Toothpicks

Straight pins

Tracing paper

Pencil

White fabric pencil

Needle and white thread or glue gun

Corrugated cardboard covered with wax paper

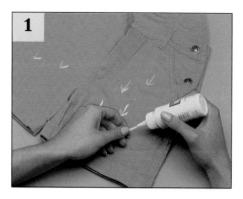

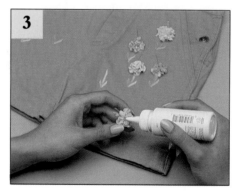

1. Beginners are advised to slip garment over covered cardboard, though the cardboard is not visible in this photo. Cut chartreuse satin ribbon on a slant into 7 lengths at 3/4-inch each for stems and 18 lengths at 1/2-inch each for leaves. Stems are placed vertically onto the garment with two leaves angled in a V-shape at the bottom of each stem. Arrange five stems with accompanying leaves on right leg and two stems with leaves on bib as shown in photo at left. Arrange four remaining leaves into two V's to make blades of grass on left leg. Dip toothpick into fabric glue to coat backs of stems and leaves, beginning with those at bottom of garment and working your way to the top.

2. Cut pink, blue, and yellow crinkled ribbon into 3-inch lengths, two for each color. To form a flower, bend one end of crinkled ribbon down about 1/4 inch and tightly roll the rest of ribbon around this end. To hold ribbon in roll, insert straight pin into outside end of ribbon and through the roll, coming out through the opposite side of roll. Repeat this step with each of the remaining 3-inch ribbon lengths.

3. Completely cover one side of rolled ribbon with fabric glue. Glue rolled-ribbon flower to top of a stem on garment, holding in place with two straight pins stuck through the flower, through the garment, and into cardboard (if using it). Do not remove pins until glue has completely dried. Glue remaining rolled-ribbon flowers to garment.

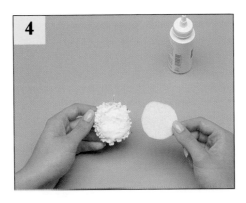

Create this design on different types of garments. Consider making a coordinated outfit featuring a cotton knit skirt and top decorated in crinkled-ribbon flowers, with the sheep grazing on the crown of a matching sun hat. For each additional flower, increase satin ribbon length by 1½ inches and crinkled ribbon by 3 inches.

4. To make sheep, roll up entire piece of white crinkled ribbon as described in Step 2. Stick several pins through roll to hold it together. Cut a circle of white felt slightly smaller than the size of rolled ribbon (about 2 ½ inches in diameter). Completely cover one side of rolled ribbon with fabric glue. Place felt circle over glue side of rolled ribbon. Set aside to dry.

5. Draw sheep's ear and leg patterns onto tracing paper and cut out. Using pattern, trace ears and legs onto black felt with white fabric pencil and cut out. When the white rolled ribbon representing the sheep's body is completely dry, flip over with felt side down on table. Position ears in center of sheep's body and position legs under bottom edge of body, as pictured. Place button below ears for sheep's face. Spread fabric glue evenly over back of ears and glue on body of sheep. Squeeze a small circle of fabric glue below ears. Place shank of button into glue. Allow to dry. Spread glue on top of legs and affix them to felt side of sheep's body near the bottom.

6. Attach safety pin to back of sheep either by sewing into place with white thread or by gluing with hot glue. Attach sheep button to bibs on left leg as shown.

Ribbon Roundup

ADVANCED

Kids love to use buttons, pins, decorative fabric, or other materials to make their denim jackets unique expressions of their individuality. Help your teens express themselves with this bold use of colored ribbon.

What You'll Need

Denim jeans and jacket

6 different colors each of ⅜ inch wide and ⅝ inch wide neon-colored satin ribbon. To determine quantity of ribbon needed, estimate 1½ yards per 3 running inches along leg, jacket front, and jacket yoke.

Double-sided fusible webbing, 17 inches wide by length of jeans leg. This should allow enough for both jeans and jacket.

10 to 15 yards ½-inch-wide double-sided fusible webbing for seam allowances

Tracing paper

Box of straight pins

Pencil

Ruler

Scissors

Water soluble pen

Iron and ironing board

Seam sealant (optional)

Fabric glue (optional)

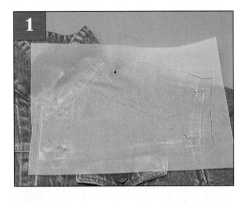

1. Pin a piece of tracing paper on the jacket or jeans and trace the general shape of the area to be covered with ribbon, allowing about a ½-inch overlap on all sides. Draw diagonal lines at right angles to each other in the direction you want the ribbons to follow. This mark will serve as your starting point for placing the ribbons.

2. Remove tracing from jacket, and straighten edges with a ruler. Trace this shape onto a sheet of fusible webbing and cut. Cut two of this shape, one a mirror image of the other. (In terms of the different shapes involved, follow the shape of the jacket for the yoke shape. The vertical strips on the front of the jacket we used measure 3½×13 inches; the pants leg strips measure 3½ × 36 inches.) On the adhesive side of pattern, using a water soluble pen, carefully—without ripping the adhesive—draw a cross at right angles to each other in the direction you want the ribbons to run, just as in Step 1.

3. Place fusible webbing pattern on ironing board, adhesive side up. Selecting colors and widths at random, cut several pieces of ribbon long enough to cover length of pattern. Begin placement of ribbons on pattern at marked cross, working your way to the ends. Using straight pins, pin ribbons to ironing board as you cover pattern. (Some may find pinning one end of the ribbons will be sufficient to hold them in place.) Continue to cut ribbons in random colors and widths and pin to board until pattern is covered. Ribbons for yoke pattern will be varying lengths. Ours were cut 4 to 6 inches long. Ribbons for vertical strips on jacket and pants will all be the same length. Ours were cut 6 inches long.

4. Cut a few ribbons to cover length of pattern in opposite direction. Because the pattern is covered with ribbons at this point, refer to marked cross on tracing paper to position ribbons correctly. Beginning at center, weave a ribbon under and over each pinned ribbon. Keep all ribbons flat and at right angles. Also make sure they cover entire pattern.

5. When all vertical and horizontal ribbons are woven in place, fuse ribbon to web, carefully removing pins as you press. Caution: Follow manufacturer's instructions for fusing. Do not allow temperature of iron to exceed suitable temperature for ribbons. Be especially cautious when using silk, lightweight, or finely printed ribbon. Too high of a temperature can cause too much adhesive to bond to ribbons. Once fused, turn ribbon assembly over and fuse again on paper side. Cut off all ribbon tails along edge of paper, then remove paper backing.

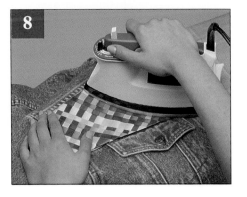

6. With right sides facing up, place ribbon fabric over area of denim to be covered. (For the jacket yoke, place appropriate ribbon fabric over yoke, mark where the button hole should be, and cut a slit in the ribbon fabric for the button hole. If desired, use seam sealant to stop fraying where ribbon fabric was slit. Return ribbon fabric to yoke.) Turn under and pin ½-inch seam allowance on all edges, but do not pin ribbon to denim.

7. Remove ribbon fabric from denim. With wrong side of ribbon fabric facing up, fuse webbing strips to all edges of seam allowances. Fuse only seam allowances, do not allow iron to touch center fused area of ribbon fabric. Remove paper backing.

8. Return ribbon fabric to denim and iron over entire area, fusing ribbon fabric to area. Repeat for all ribbon fabric pieces. A little dab of fabric glue may help to hold trouble spots.

Beaded Denim

BEGINNER

The diverse types of clothing available in denim makes it the perfect fabric to experiment with—as shown in this shirt and hat ensemble.

What You'll Need

SHIRT

Sleeveless shirt with collar

2 cranberry donut beads, 20mm each

1 frosted cobalt donut bead, 30mm

1 teal donut bead, 40mm

2 amber cushion beads, 14 × 8.5mm each

2 cinnabar cushion beads, 18 × 11mm each

1 denim cushion bead, 22 × 13.5mm

1 frosted crystal barrel bead, 10 × 9mm

2 amethyst barrel beads, 14 × 12.5mm each

1 tiger coral barrel bead, 19 × 17mm

1 bone hairpipe bead, 38 × 10mm

Fabric glue

Black cotton embroidery floss and embroidery needle

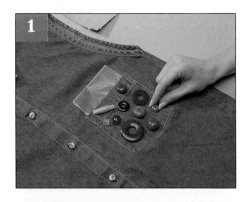

1. Using fabric glue, glue back side of beads and adhere to pocket and collar of shirt. Put wax paper inside pocket to prevent glue from leaking. Refer to finished photo for placement of beads. Let glue dry 24 hours.(The purpose of the glue is to hold the beads in place.)

2. Thread six strands of embroidery floss through eye of needle and knot the ends together. When sewing barrel and hairpipe beads on the pocket and collar, start from back side of material, then push the needle up through material, and then thread it through the bead. Push needle back down through the material and out the back side. Be sure not to sew pocket or collar to shirt. Knot the end of the thread strand and then cut excess.

3. For donut and cushion beads, follow same general sewing instructions as stated in Step 2: Use six strands of floss, knot end, start at back side of collar and pocket, etc. Follow photos for decorative stitch patterns. (The purpose of sewing with the floss is decorative.)

HAT

1 frosted cobalt bead, 30mm

1 teal donut bead, 40mm

1 denim cushion bead, 22 × 13.5mm

1 bone hairpipe bead, 38 × 10mm

1 frosted crystal barrel bead, 10 × 9mm

1 tiger coral barrel bead, 19 × 17mm barrel bead

Fabric glue

Black cotton embroidery floss

Embroidery needle

Scissors

1. Using fabric glue, glue back side of beads and adhere to brim of floppy hat. Refer to photo for placement of beads. Let glue dry 24 hours.

2. As in Step 2 for shirt, thread 6 strands of embroidery floss through eye of needle and knot the end. Sew beads in place. For barrel and hairpipe beads, start from back side of brim and push needle up through brim, then thread through bead. Push needle down and out the back side of brim. Knot the end of thread strand and cut excess. For donut and cushion beads, follow same general sewing instructions: Use six strands of floss, knot end, start at back side of brim, and so forth. Follow photos for decorative stitch patterns. (This step is not pictured.)

| 40 mm donut | 30 mm donut | 20 mm donut | 22×13.5mm cushion | 18×11mm cushion | 14×8.5mm cushion | 19×17mm barrel | 14×12.5mm barrel | 10×9mm barrel | hair pipe |

Indian Summer

When it's time to grab a mug of apple cider and enjoy a late summer sunset, you'll be glad you decorated this jacket. Put on this outerwear—with it's stylish details and distinctive look— and you'll make a statement without saying a word.

What You'll Need

Jacket

Medium or heavy weight fabric(s) with Native-American or Southwestern motifs (amount varies according to motif and jacket size)

Heavy-duty fusible webbing (enough to cover motifs)

Assorted brass charms

Dimensional black fabric paint

Industrial-strength adhesive glue

Scissors

Straight pins

Needle

Black thread

Iron and ironing board

1. Select area of fabric that you will use on jacket. Following manufacturer's instructions, iron fusible webbing to wrong side of fabric. Cut out the designs you will be using and peel off paper backing.

2. Work with placement of appliqués until you are satisfied with design. To achieve desired look, you may need to piece together different areas of the fabric as shown. After you have your fabric arranged on the front of the jacket, pin pieces in position. Repeat this step on back of jacket.

3. Iron fabric pieces in place, removing pins as you go. Rub hand over appliqués to make sure edges are secured. Iron again if necessary, though ironing should take no longer than three to seven seconds. Trace around appliqués with black dimensional paint to help secure edges and to give a finished look. Repeat this step on back of jacket.

TIP

For the appliquéd areas, using ready-made panels of appliqués is not necessary; any patterned fabric is potentially usable. Let your creative energy flow!

4. Lay the jacket flat. Arrange charms on collar. Draw an imaginary line from the pocket buttons down the front, and place charms on line. Using the needle and thread, sew charms in place. Sew a row of charms above the bottom edge of jacket, alternating charms around the entire jacket. You can also set off fabric appliqués by adding well-placed charms. Repeat this step on back of jacket. (This step is not pictured.)

5. To attach charms to buttons, use a toothpick to apply industrial strength adhesive glue to the back side of charms. Make sure the charms used on the buttons do not interfere with the buttonhole.

Pumpkin Pockets and Silly Socklets

INTERMEDIATE

This Halloween, your toddler can tote around a pumpkin pal and a gaggle of ghosts in this wacky wearable. Add the matching pumpkin purse for a unique kiddy ensemble.

What You'll Need

1 pair bib overalls

Infant terry socks

Three 3 × 36-inch strips of any color fabric

4 squares orange or gold felt

2 squares black felt

1 yard fusible webbing

½ yard orange ribbon, ¼ inch wide

2 overall-type buttons

Fabric paint in shiny black, shiny orange and/or smoky topaz, and red

Small flat paint brush

Scissors

Safety pins

Needle

Thread to match

Iron and ironing board

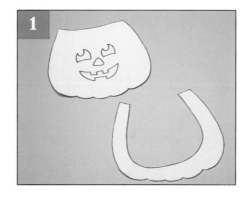

1. Trace patterns directly onto paper side of fusible webbing. (Patterns can be found on page 164.) Cut only around the outside of the shapes. Do not cut out the facial features.

2. For the pocket, there will be three layers of felt. First, following manufacturer's instructions, iron pumpkin face cut from fusible webbing onto orange felt. Then, cut out shape and facial features. Peel off paper backing and fuse orange pumpkin shape to black felt. Cut out around the outside of the pumpkin shape.

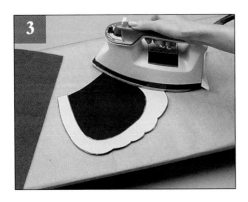

3. Iron U-shaped piece of fusible webbing to black side of pumpkin. Peel off paper backing and fuse an orange felt square to pumpkin. Iron with the black side up. Cut out around the outside of the pumpkin shape.

4. To make button holes, position pumpkin face over bib on overalls, just covering top edge. Mark button placement. Slit triple layers of pumpkin vertically, starting ½ inch from top. Make slits just long enough for buttons to fit through.

5. We outlined facial features in black fabric paint. To provide accent, we painted pumpkin ridges in smoky topaz. (Shiny orange also works well.) Using the red fabric paint, we dry brushed cheeks. Feel free to design your own eyelashes, smile lines, or other accents. Let dry and attach to overalls.

6. To make ghost puppets, use infant terry socks. Dry brush red fabric paint on cheek area. Paint eyes, nose, and mouth with black fabric paint. Feel free to improvise. Let dry. Make a simple bow from orange ribbon and sew on ghost at chin or top of head. Puppets go in pockets of bib overalls and in the pumpkin pocket attached to the front. Remove ghosts and pumpkin pocket before laundering.

7. To make purse, repeat Steps 1-4 for pumpkin body. Paint features on purse following directions in Step 5 to match pumpkin pocket. (This step is not pictured.)

8. To make fabric strap for purse, use three 3 × 36-inch strips of fabric. Fold raw edges in and safety pin all three ends together at one end. Braid entire length, enclosing raw edges as you braid. Safety pin at end of braid.

9. Bend or fold strap in half. Position strap on back of pumpkin purse and mark strap at desired length. Sew material strands together at marks. Attach a button at each mark. Trim ends as desired. Fill purse with a ghost.

Button Down

BEGINNER

Button covers are easy-to-make accessories that add a touch of class to any blouse. Here, pearl button covers and a few floral motifs transform this denim shirt into a dressy wearable.

What You'll Need

Short-sleeve shirt

Fabric (we used a floral print, a striped floral print combination, and a black print with white dots)

Pearl-colored fabric paint

6 button-cover findings

6 buttons (we used 2 small black and 4 large black)

6 half-pearl button charms

Scissors

Ruler

Marking pen

Fabric glue

Crafters cement or hot melt glue

Straight pins

Craft stick or small paint brush

Shirt board

Craft paper to cover work surface

1. Cut out the following motifs from fabric: For pockets, cut two 2 × 2½-inch rectangles from floral fabric and two 1-inch diamond shapes from the black and white fabric. For collar, cut two oval shapes from floral fabric. For cuffs and button hole flap, cut three 16-inch stripes from floral and striped fabric.

2. Place motifs upside down on wax paper. Squeeze fabric glue on wrong side and spread with craft stick or small paint brush. Make sure to get glue all the way to edges. Place shirt on shirt board and lay flat on work surface. Glue motifs to shirt collar and pockets. Press in place with fingers.

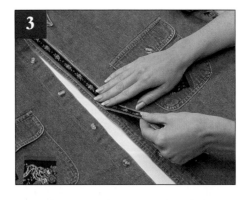

3. Glue fabric stripes around cuffs and down center of button hole cuff. Make sure shirt is unbuttoned with both sides separated so that glue does not seep through button holes and onto back of shirt. Pin in place with straight pins to secure while glue dries. Let dry 24 hours.

4. Outline motifs with pearl fabric paint. Gently squeeze a thin line of fabric paint around edges. Highlight some details inside motifs if desired.

5. Cut slits with scissors through fabric over button holes. Button shirt.

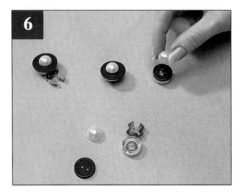

6. For button covers, glue black button to button cover findings. Glue half-pearl button charms to buttons. Slide button cover over button.

Traveler's Jacket

ADVANCED

By using photo-transfer medium, you can recycle your favorite postcards onto a denim jacket for a one-of-a-kind souvenir of your favorite vacation site. Whether you prefer the tropical delights of Florida or the misty mountains of Montana, your jacket will be a reflection of your personality.

What You'll Need

Denim jacket (stonewashed is best)

½ yard medium-weight white cotton or cotton blend fabric

Mirror-image color photocopies of about 6 postcards and the map of the state (one of our postcards had several small photos on it that we cut apart and used separately)

Dimensional glitter paint (we used glittering gold platinum)

Round faceted acrylic gemstones to cover buttons or snaps on jacket (ours are 15mm)

Assortment of faceted acrylic gemstones

Assortment of brass charms

Photo-transfer medium

Fusible webbing

Scissors

Wax paper

1-inch sponge brush

Rolling pin

Iron and ironing board

Pressing cloth

Disappearing-ink pen

Washable glue

Palette

Industrial-strength adhesive

Toothpicks

Pliers

1. Tentatively plan the placement of postcards and map on your jacket. Do this before you have your copies made so you know what you will need. After photocopying your postcards and map, trim white edges from postcard photocopies as shown. If you included a postcard with several photos on it that you want to use individually, cut them apart. Do not trim photocopy of state map. Cut white fabric into four rectangles about 9 × 12 inches as shown. These will be easier to work with than one long strip of fabric. Place each piece of white fabric on a sheet of wax paper.

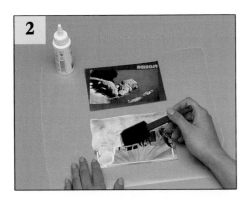

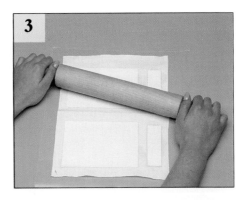

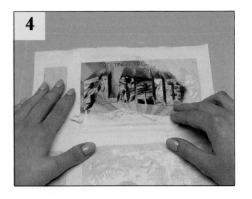

2. Lay photocopies face up on separate sheets of wax paper. Working on one copy at a time, apply a thick layer of transfer medium with finger or sponge brush. Be sure all edges and corners have been covered.

3. Place copy face down on white fabric. Smooth with fingers and rolling pin, making sure to remove any air bubbles. If any transfer medium is pressed out of sides, wipe it up immediately. Leave about an inch of fabric border around all copies. Dry flat for 24 hours. After 24 hours, remove fabric from wax paper and heat-set both sides of transfers for 30 seconds using a pressing cloth and a dry iron on a wool setting. Let cool.

4. Soak transfers in water for 30 to 60 minutes. Remove from water. Squeeze excess water from fabric as much as possible, but do not wring transfer area. Lay fabric on a clean, flat surface. Using your fingers, gently rub paper backing. Work from the center of the transfer to the outside edges. When you have removed the first layer of paper, return fabric to water to soak for another 15 minutes. Remove from water, repeating process until all paper particles have been removed. Be especially careful when rubbing edges so as not to tear the transfer. Let fabric dry flat. (Transfers may appear cloudy. They will become more defined when washable glue is applied later, but they will never be as clear as the original.)

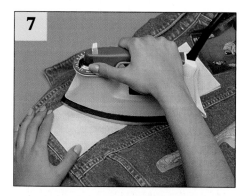

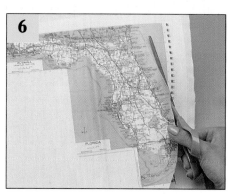

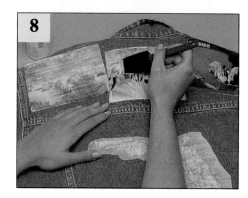

5. Cut one rectangle of fusible webbing slightly smaller than each piece of fabric. When all paper particles have been removed and fabric is dry, follow manufacturer's instructions and fuse webbing to back of fabric.

6. Using a disappearing-ink pen, draw a line just outside the state's borders on the map. Cut on the line. Cut out postcards on edges of transfers.

7. Remove paper backing from adhesive on the back of transfers. On a hard surface (not a padded ironing board cover), arrange photo transfers of map and postcards as desired on jacket. Cover transfers with pieces of paper backing from iron-on adhesive, shiny side down to protect your iron and your transfer. Follow manufacturer's instructions for fusing. Iron on all transfers, front and back.

8. Pour a puddle of washable glue onto palette and use sponge brush to apply a thin, even coat to transfers on front of jacket. If some of the transfer edges are popping up, spread a small amount of glue underneath. When front is dry, repeat for the transfers on the back.

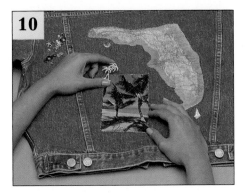

9. When glue is dry, outline cards and map with dimensional glitter paint. Be sure to keep tip of bottle on fabric. Do the front of jacket, then, when paint is dry, turn over and do the back.

10. After paint dries, arrange acrylic gemstones in desired spots on back of jacket. We used a star on the state capital, a heart on our favorite city, and various sizes and colors of round stones on different cities throughout the state. We used 15mm round stones and plastic dogwood leaves to represent oranges, and we placed 15mm stones on the back buttons. Use pliers to remove holes from brass charms, if desired. Arrange charms on back of jacket.

11. Lift up one gem or charm at a time and use a toothpick to apply industrial strength glue to backs. Work in a well ventilated area to avoid inhaling fumes from glue. To glue round gems to metal buttons, use toothpick to spread a layer of glue on the back of gem and on the top of the metal button. Allow each to dry for about ten minutes before pressing together.

12. Turn jacket over and arrange gems and charms on the front. Glue charms and gems on jacket and buttons as directed in Step 11.

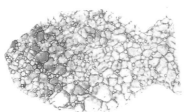

Animal
CRACKERS

Aschool of fish, a pair of fawns. From fancy fishy appliqués to flocked fowl in flight, these animals are about to overrun your wardrobe! Often adorable and great for kids, animal designs are a natural for wearables. Animal patterns are appropriate for any technique, whether it be stamping, painting, or appliqué. They can be simplified into an almost abstract motif or rendered realistically. Fish make a colorful motif for wearable projects: Your teenager will love the "Gone Fishin'" romper, while Grandma will be the envy of the beach in the "Fishy Straw Hat with Shoes." Looking for a project for that little boy who can't leave the creepy, crawly things alone? Try "The Bugs Go Marching 2 by 2." And, as the ducks fly south for the winter, stay warm in your own "Flock of Ducks" sweatsuit. Prowl through this jungle of wild wearables if you're looking for animal magnetism!

Fishy Straw Hat With Shoes

ADVANCED

Catch the colors of Siamese fighting fish from top to toe in this hat and shoes ensemble. When summer is over and the beach is closed, remove the scarf and fish pin for winter wear.

What You'll Need

Straw hat

Pair of straw shoes

9 × 54-inch silk scarf

Hot pink spray paint

Silk dyes in periwinkle, bright green, and azure blue

Blue violet acrylic paint

Sponge brush

1/4-inch shader taklon brush

2 sheets of metallic-colored plastic in green/teal/blue, 7 inches each

3 sheets of metallic-colored plastic in copper/red/blue, 7 inches each

3 large, black seed beads

Pin backing

Masking tape

Newspaper

Wax paper

Iron

Adhesive glue

2 rubber bands

Aluminum foil

Cookie sheet

Cooking spray

Tweezers

Pencil with blunt end

Knife

Permanent ink pen

Cooking pot

Scissors

Shampoo

Typing paper

1. Wash scarf in mild shampoo and rinse. Roll in towel to remove excess water. Fold scarf in half and place on wax paper. Scrunch up. Sponge green onto open ends of scarf, blue to middle, and periwinkle to folded end, overlapping colors. Squeeze together gently so colors mingle. Hang to dry. Iron to set colors.

2. Mask shoe sole sides with masking tape. Stuff insides with newspapers. Spray with hot pink paint. When dry, remove paper and tape. Paint sole sides with blue violet acrylic. Let dry.

3. Spray straw hat with hot pink paint. (This step is not pictured.)

4. Trace fish pattern onto typing paper. (Pattern can be found on page 165.) Cut out. You will need two fish facing one way and one facing the other, so trace pattern accordingly. On wrong side of plastic sheet, trace fish using permanent marker. Cut three fish bodies from green/teal/blue metallic plastic, making sure to remember that two fish face one way and one faces the other. Cut three back fins, three tails, and three eye bases from copper/red/blue metallic plastic, making sure eye base is on the gold color. Cut six gills and six front fins from copper/red/blue metallic plastic.

5. Preheat oven to 225 degrees. Cover cookie sheet with aluminum foil. Spray foil with cooking spray. Place fish body face up on foil. Place back fins, tail, and one front fin under body. Place other front fin, eye base, and one gill on top of fish body. See photo for correct placement of fish parts. Put in oven. Remove from oven when pieces are warm enough to adhere together.

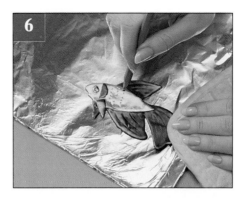

6. Center bead on eye and press imprint of bead. Remove bead. Detail lines on fins with knife. Detail scale marks with blunt pencil as shown. While fish is still pliable, cover shoe front with a piece of aluminum foil and press fish over shoe to fit shoe curve. Allow fish to harden in curved shape. Repeat steps to make the other two fish. Curve one facing the opposite direction for opposite shoe. Leave one fish flat.

7. Heat water to simmer, adding a few drops of oil. Place fin in water and shape into soft curves. Place tail into water and shape into soft curves. Repeat for other two fish.

8. Heat tweezers to make lines in second gill. Smooth over first gill with fingers. Add indent lines on gill beside eye with knife. Repeat for other two fish.

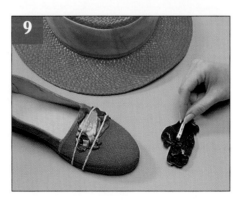

9. Wash and dry fish. With adhesive, glue eyes in place. Glue curved fish to shoes, using rubber bands to keep fish in place on shoe while adhesive is drying. Let dry overnight. Glue pin backing to flat fish. Tie scarf around hat. Pin hat brim up with fish pin after allowing glue to dry thoroughly.

The Bugs Go Marching 2 by 2

BEGINNER

Kids are crazy about stickers. Take advantage of the current craze by incorporating them into this simple wearable-art project. Let your little one get involved by having him or her pick the stickers they want on their shoes.

What You'll Need

Canvas tennis shoes and cotton baseball-style cap

Stickers

Washable fabric glue

1-inch sponge brush

Masking tape

Palette

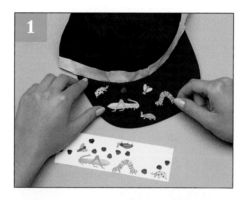

1. Prepare shoes and cap by washing and drying. (Air dry the cap.) Remove shoelaces from the shoes. Put strip of masking tape around cap where the bill is attached. Arrange stickers on shoes and bill of cap, moving them around until you are satisfied with their placement.

2. Pour a puddle of washable glue onto the palette. Using your finger, spread glue in a thin layer on one shoe at a time. Lift edges of stickers and spread glue under stickers, on bottom of stickers, and on top of stickers. Cover entire bill of cap and canvas surface of shoes with glue. Do not put glue onto the tongues of the shoes. The surface of the bill and shoes will have a cloudy appearance while the glue is wet.

3. Let glue dry until it is clear but still tacky. (Drying time varies according to season and temperature.) Use sponge brush to apply a thin, even coat of glue over entire area. Press down any sticker edges that have popped up. If small bubbles appear when you are applying glue, brush until they disappear because the bubbles will not dry clear. Repeat drying time and apply a third coat of glue with the sponge brush. The shoes need at least three coats of glue, while the cap can get by with two. Let shoes and cap dry thoroughly before wearing.

Gone Fishin'

INTERMEDIATE

Fusible webbing has made possible a variety of craft ideas that are simple yet quite dazzling. This project features brightly colored fish designs that were cut from fabric and then fused onto a simple, inexpensive white romper.

What You'll Need

One-piece romper in stretch or woven fabric in light, solid color

1 to 2 yards brightly colored, lightweight, firmly woven print fabric (no knits or stretch material). Fabric should feature large individual motifs with no overlapping.

Buttons coordinated to match fabric

1 to 2 yards fusible webbing

Pencil

Scissors

Tape measure

Iron and ironing board

Note: Before cutting design motifs from fabric, reserve enough fabric for the sash by cutting two 6 × 30-inch lengths. Also cut three ½ × 6-inch lengths and two ½ × 30-inch lengths of fusible webbing.

1. Cut a motif from the fabric, allowing at least a ½-inch border around the perimeter of the design. Place fusible webbing on table, with the paper side up. Place fabric motif on paper with the right side down. Trace along fabric edge onto paper. Cut fusible webbing ⅛ inch to ¼ inch inside of traced line.

2. Following manufacturer's instructions, fuse webbing to wrong side of fabric motif. Cutting through paper-backed webbing and fabric, cut motif along design lines.

3. Remove paper backing from motif. Position webbed-backed motif on romper and fuse following manufacturer's instructions. It is suggested that you prepare all motifs with webbing, cut them out, determine their position on the romper, and then fuse them one at a time. Replace romper buttons with coordinating buttons.

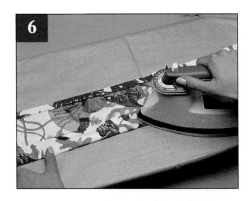

TIP

The matching sash constructed via fusible webbing turns this project from "Beginner" to "Intermediate." Beginning crafters may want to exclude the matching sash, opting to purchase a belt in a coordinating color.

4. For the sash, make sure you have reserved two 6 × 30-inch lengths of fabric. Turn under and press ½ inch on one short end of one length. Following manufacturer's instructions, apply fusible webbing strip to edge that is folded under (seam allowance) and remove paper backing. Fuse to short end of second 6 × 30-inch fabric length, thereby connecting both lengths of fabric. (Note: Do not fold under and press end of second fabric strip. See photo.)

5. Turn under and press ½ inch on one long edge and on both short ends of seamed sash. Apply fusible webbing to all three folded edges (seam allowances) and then remove paper backing.

6. Turn under and press 1½ inches along long unfolded edge. Avoid allowing iron to touch any exposed adhesive from the webbing.

7. Lay sash on ironing surface so that long, folded, webbed edge is on top, with adhesive face up. Fold top edge over 1¼ inches, which should overlap cut edge of bottom fold. Press with iron to fuse.

A Flock of Ducks

INTERMEDIATE

What better way to use flocking than to make a flock of ducks. You'll love how fast this project goes as it begins to fit together like a jigsaw puzzle.

What You'll Need

Gray or ash sweatshirt and sweatpants, prewashed with no fabric softener

Iron-on flocking sheets in black, yellow, white, cardinal red, brown, aqua, green, and orange

Bronze dimensional fabric paint

Transfer paper

Tracing paper

Stylis

Scissors

Iron

Shirt board

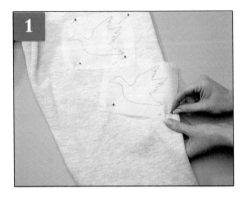

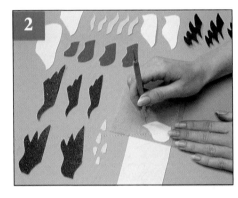

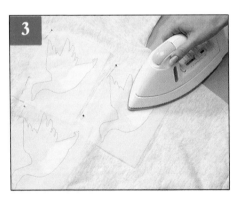

1. Trace the outlines of three large and two small ducks onto tracing paper. (Pattern can be found on page 165.) Cut out. Pin onto shirt and pants, positioning as illustrated. Try on outfit. Reposition ducks if necessary.

2. Trace all interior lines onto one large duck and one small duck. Usingthese paper patterns, transfer each duck part to back of appropriately colored flocked paper with transfer paper and stylus. Follow diagram on page 165. You may cut out each individual duck part from paper pattern and trace onto flocked paper, or keep the duck pattern intact and trace each part from intact drawing. (You will need an intact duck tracing to use as a guide in the next step.) Cut enough of each part to make three large ducks and two small. Set aside the eyes, feet, and neck rings.

3. For the shirt, arrange the three large white body pieces, using tracing paper guides as shown. Following manufacturer's directions, iron on white body pieces. Remove guides.

4. Continue ironing on duck pieces as you fit them together in jigsaw fashion.

5. Iron on eyes, neck rings, and feet, using tracing paper between the flocked area and the iron. Iron shirt inside out to make sure flocking adheres.

6. Place shirt on shirt board. Fold sleeves or tape in back to make sure shirt is smooth on front. Outline all pieces with dimensional paint. Dot eye center. Dry flat.

7. Proceed with pants as directed for shirt, using small ducks. (This step is not pictured.)

Neon Fish and Waves

BEGINNER

Sponge-print t-shirts are simple to design and easy to produce. This t-shirt and matching visor remind us of a day at the beach or a fabulous vacation. The bright colors and ocean motifs make the t-shirt a perfect choice to wear over a bathing suit, while the visor will help protect your child from too much sun.

What You'll Need

White t-shirt

Dimensional fabric paint in bright blue, neon pink, and neon green

White plastic visor

Shirt board

Yardstick

Disappearing-ink pen

White paper for tracing patterns

Pencil

Scissors

Compressed sponge

Palette

Wax paper

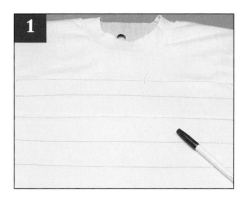

1. Put t-shirt on shirt board. To make guidelines for sponge prints, place yardstick across shirt about 2 inches below bottom of neckline. With a disappearing-ink pen, make two lines, one above and one below yardstick. (The lines should be about 1¼ inches apart.) Make four more lines each about 1½ inches below the previous one. Then make one last line 1¼ inch (approximate width of yardstick) below those. There should be a total of seven lines drawn across the shirt front.

2. Trace fish and wave patterns onto white paper and cut out. (Patterns can be found on page 162.) Draw around patterns onto compressed sponge, once for wave and twice for fish. Cut out. Moisten sponges and squeeze out all excess water.

3. Squirt blue paint onto palette in a puddle about the size of the wave sponge. Dip wave sponge in paint, dab off excess on clean area of palette, and press sponge gently to center of shirt just slightly above the top guideline. Then, working from the center, match edge of sponge with edge of first printed wave to continue row of waves. Make an equal number of waves on each side of first wave. Repeat for second row of waves, aligning each print with the corresponding wave in the row above. Place second row of waves just above the second line.

TIP

To make a sponge-print shirt even easier, purchase pre-cut sponges. Plan your shirt design around the sponge shapes you find. Pre-cut sponges come in a variety of simple, basic shapes, including stars, anchors, Christmas trees, etc. Your shirt designs can make use of these sponges in either a symmetrical or random fashion.

4. Squirt puddles of neon green and neon pink paint onto palettes. Dip one fish sponge into pink paint, dab off excess, and press to shirt just above the third line, with fish facing left. Using other fish sponge, dip into green paint, dab off excess, and make a green fish print about ⅛ inch to each side of center fish. Green fish should face right. Continue by making pink fish on each side of green ones. Make another row of fish below, starting with the green fish in the center. Make third row of fish identical to first row. Complete shirt by using wave sponge and blue paint to make two more rows of waves. (Note: On shirt, all pink fish face left, and all green fish face right.)

5. To paint the visor, place it on wax paper. Starting in center and working out toward the back, make a row of waves at the top of the visor curving to conform to shape. Under the waves in the center of the visor, make a green fish facing left. Make pink fish on each side, facing right. Curve around with pink fish to conform to visor shape. Hold visor firmly on wax paper and make another row of waves below fish, curving completely around visor bill. Run off edge onto wax paper if necessary. (Note: On visor, pink fish face right, and green fish face left.)

Forest Interlude

You don't have to be an expert painter to master this peaceful forest scene. Acrylic paints blend together on a moistened fabric to achieve the watercolor look.

What You'll Need

Aqua t-shirt

Acrylic colors in hansa yellow light, napthol red light, dioxazine purple, titanium white, phtahlo blue, and burnt sienna

Iridescent acrylic colors in white, gold, crimson, and green

Black iron-on transfer pen

Black fabric marker (we used a #5)

1-inch flat brush

#10, #4, and #1 round brushes

Disposable palette

Brush tub

Masking tape

Heat resistant tape

Tracing paper

Pencil

Spray bottle

Shirt board

Iron

Paper towels

1. Tape tracing paper over one side of pattern. Trace pattern with iron-on pen, omitting register marks.(Pattern can be found on pages 166 and 167.) Trace register marks (asterisks) with pencil. Trace second half of pattern, using register marks as guides.

2. Place shirt on shirt board with front on back of board so that wax from the board will not melt when ironing. Smooth and tape sleeves and bottom to back with masking tape. With heat-resistant tape, tape pattern onto shirt so trees are vertical. Iron pattern onto shirt. Remove shirt and put it on the front of the shirt board, smoothing and taping as before.

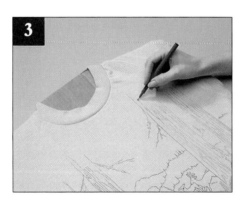

3. Retrace lines with permanent marker. Add height to trees and extend shrubs at sides.

4. Prepare palette with large dollops of burnt sienna, titanium white, hansa yellow, phthalo blue, dioxazine purple, and iridescent green in paint wells. Mix a tiny amount of blue with the yellow, for a yellow-green color. Add a healthy amount of water to each color with a spray bottle, striving for a very thin, watercolor consistency. Stir until mixed well. Add small amounts of the remaining colors in paint wells. Mix to watercolor consistency as each color is needed. (This step is not pictured.)

Color Directions

SKY: Begin by painting white clouds about 5 inches above mountains, working down both sides. Paint blue above clouds, blending into white. Leave collar unpainted.

LEFT MOUNTAINS: Top of mountains should be purple, leaving areas near shrubbery clear.

RIGHT MOUNTAINS: These are purple and blue mixed, leaving areas near shrubbery clear.

SMALL TREE: The trees feature yellow-green leaves, and a burnt sienna trunk and limbs.

CENTER AREA: Bushes just left of deer are green. If necessary, add blue to yellow-green to make green. For back bushes, add more blue for a blue-green color. Carry these colors around the trees.

PATH: Dots of napthol red followed by mixture of purple/iridescent crimson make up the path. Blend with iridescent gold and a touch of green.

DEER: The deer have iridescent white chests, with a mixture of burnt sienna and iridescent gold for the bodies.

FERN AREAS: Ferns are iridescent green with yellow-green around them. Blend a touch of iridescent green and red into parts of foreground.

TREE IVY: The ivy consists of both napthol red and crimson.

LARGE TREES: These trees have burnt sienna trunks. Paint past the ink lines of the trees with no tops. Use iridescent green for pine needles of trees.

RHODODENDRONS: Use iridescent green leaves with touches of iridescent gold. Use purple blended with iridescent crimson for center of flowers and area around bush. Use iridescent crimson and white mixed with napthol red for main part of flowers. Include iridescent white on edges. Use burnt sienna blended with iridescent gold for stems.

5. Prop up shirt board with books or against a wall. Lightly spray shirt front with water. Shirt should remain moist (but not soaked) throughout painting. Begin painting. Paint should blend together, moving outside the black lines for a water-color effect. Scrub colors into fabric, using the larger brush for larger areas and the smaller brushes for smaller areas. Follow color suggestions described at left. Also use photos on page 149 as a guide.

6. When shirt is almost dry, repaint any colors that need emphasis. When shirt is completely dry, go over any black lines that need to be defined.

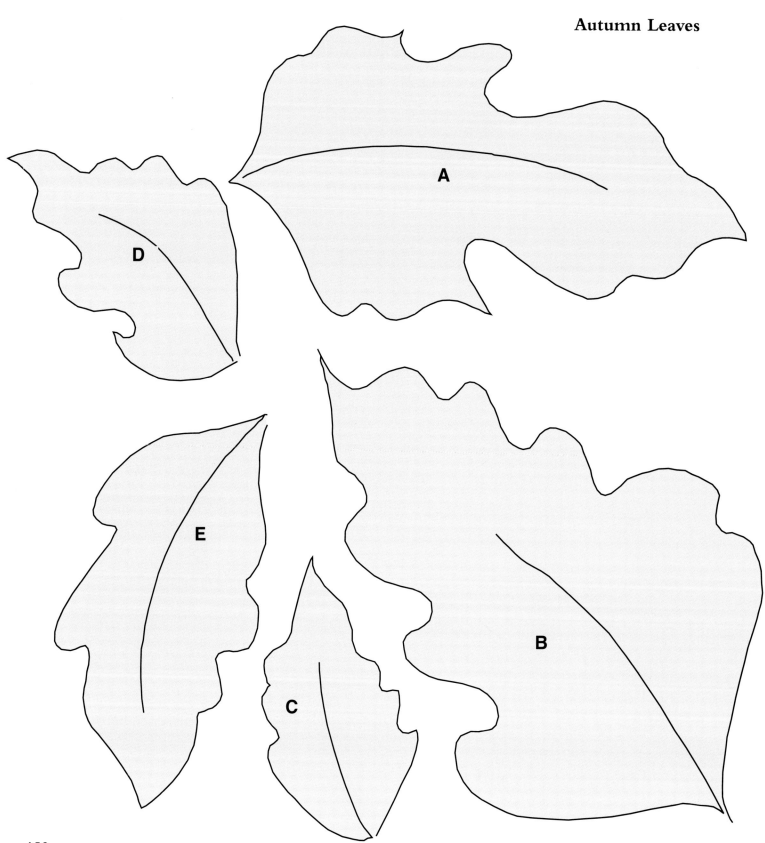

Circle of Diamonds

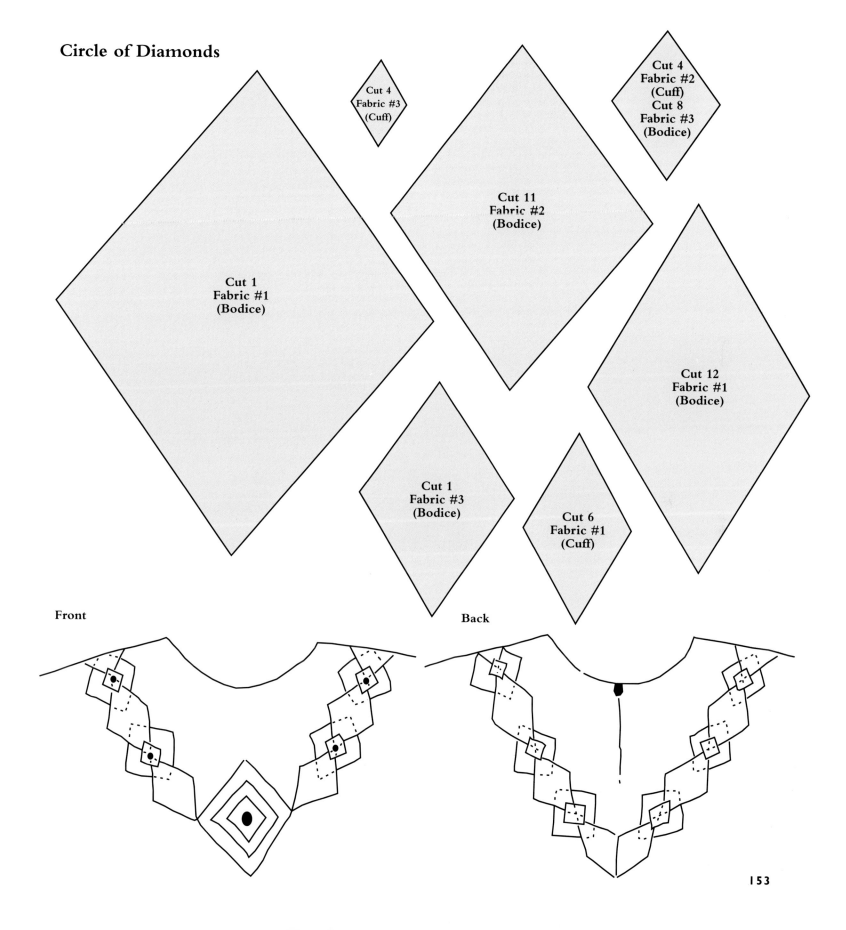

Cut 4
Fabric #3
(Cuff)

Cut 4
Fabric #2
(Cuff)
Cut 8
Fabric #3
(Bodice)

Cut 11
Fabric #2
(Bodice)

Cut 1
Fabric #1
(Bodice)

Cut 12
Fabric #1
(Bodice)

Cut 1
Fabric #3
(Bodice)

Cut 6
Fabric #1
(Cuff)

Front

Back

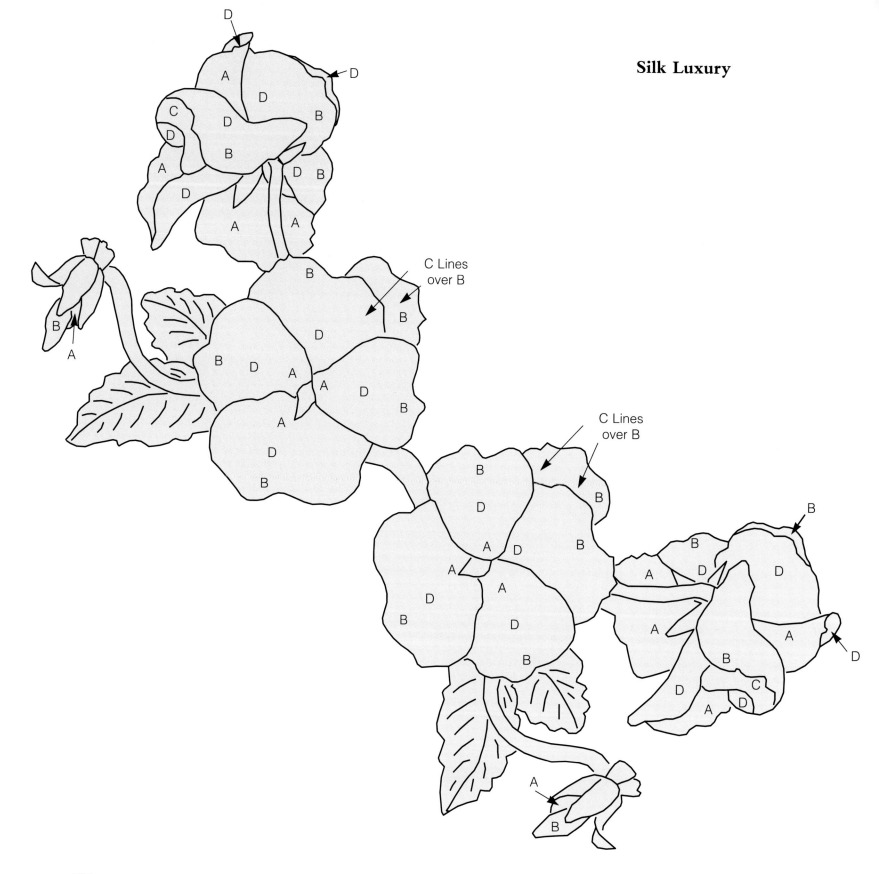

Silk Luxury

Sparkling Lights

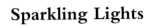

**Lacy Angel
Christmas Vest**

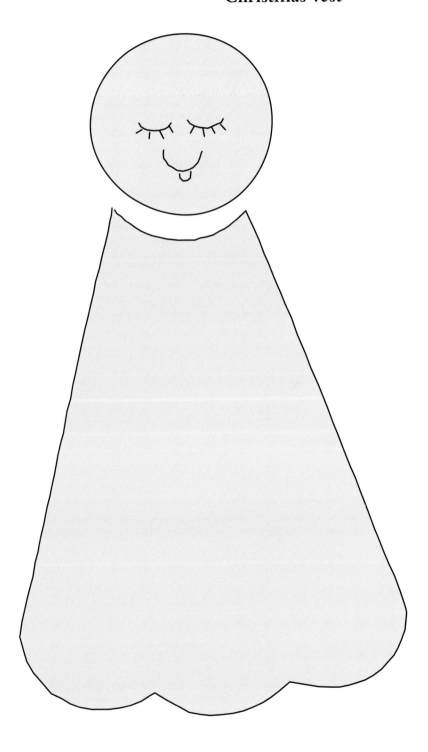

Jumper Jive

Circle Pattern for
Yo-Yo Flowers and
Leaves

Cut 9 Flowers
Cut 10 Leaves

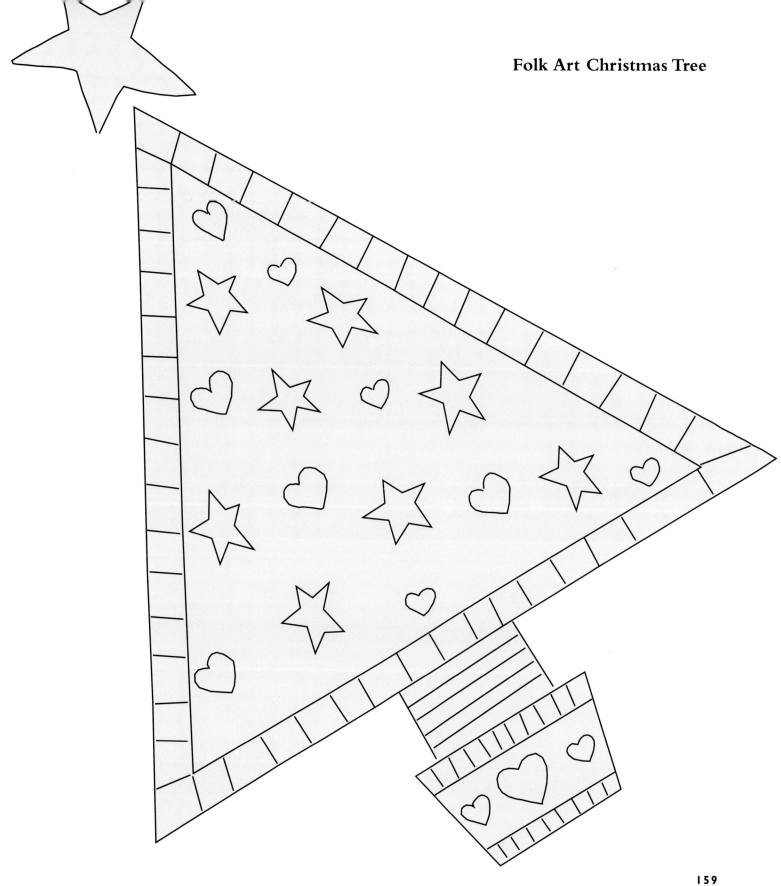

Folk Art Christmas Tree

Poinsettia Cardigan

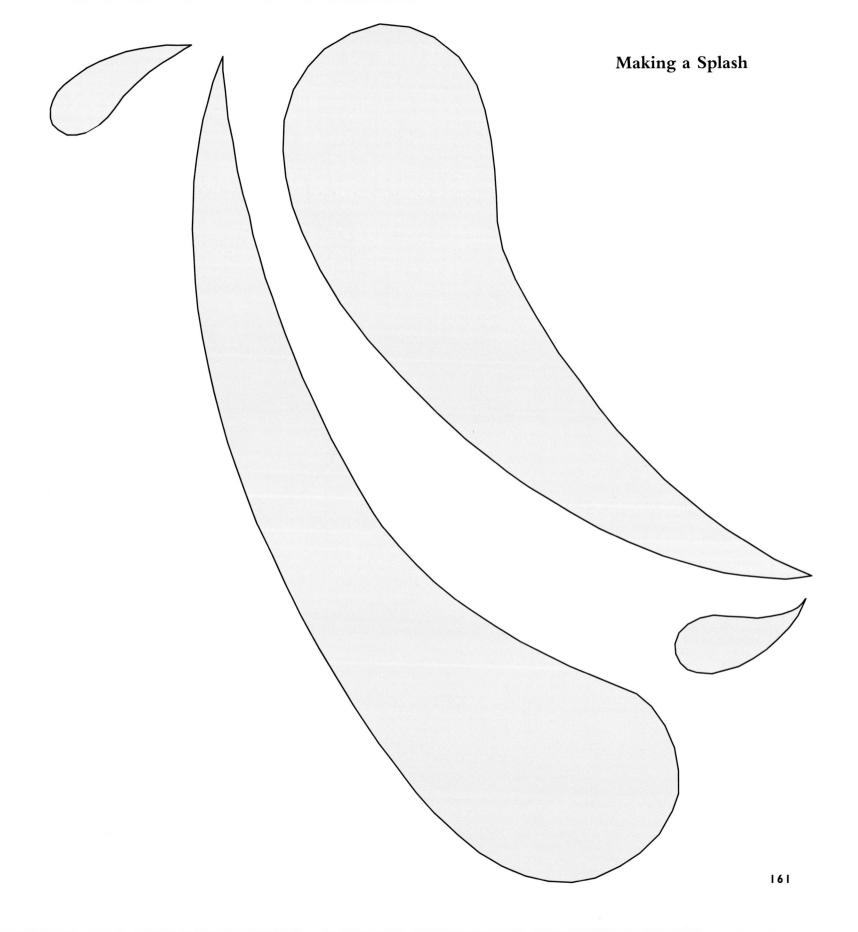

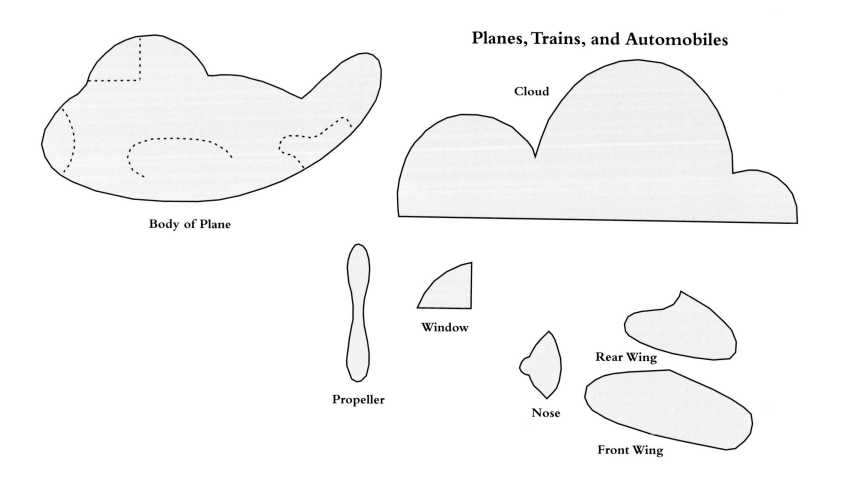

Planes, Trains, and Automobiles

Body of Plane

Cloud

Propeller

Window

Nose

Rear Wing

Front Wing

Neon Fish and Waves

Finished Plane

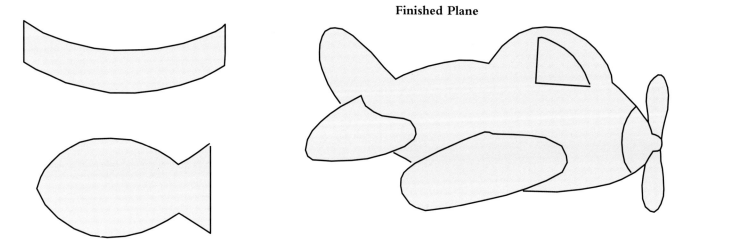

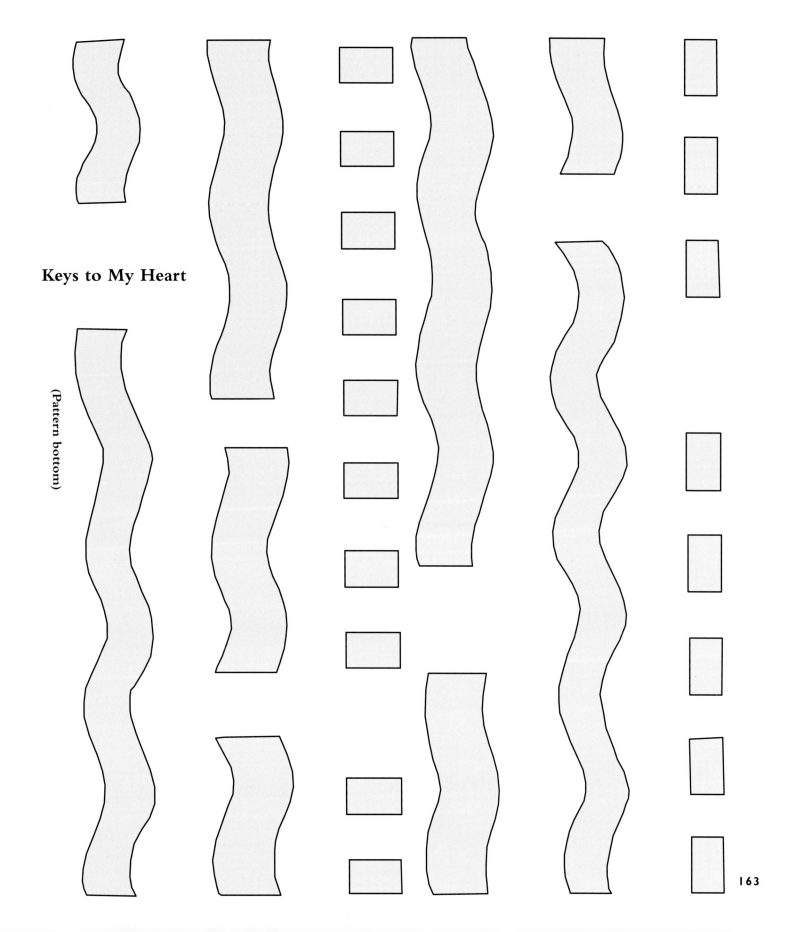

Keys to My Heart

(Pattern bottom)

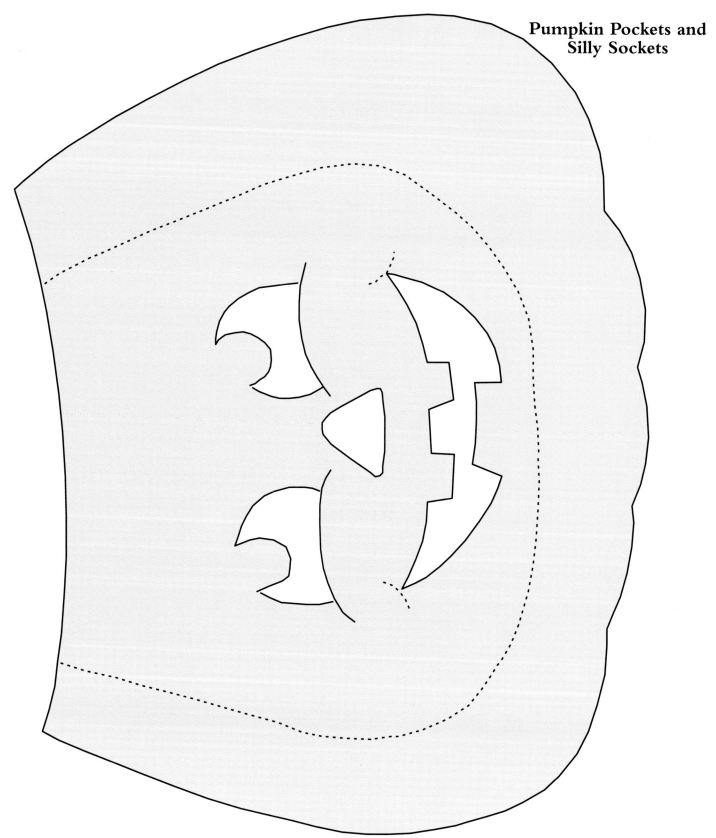

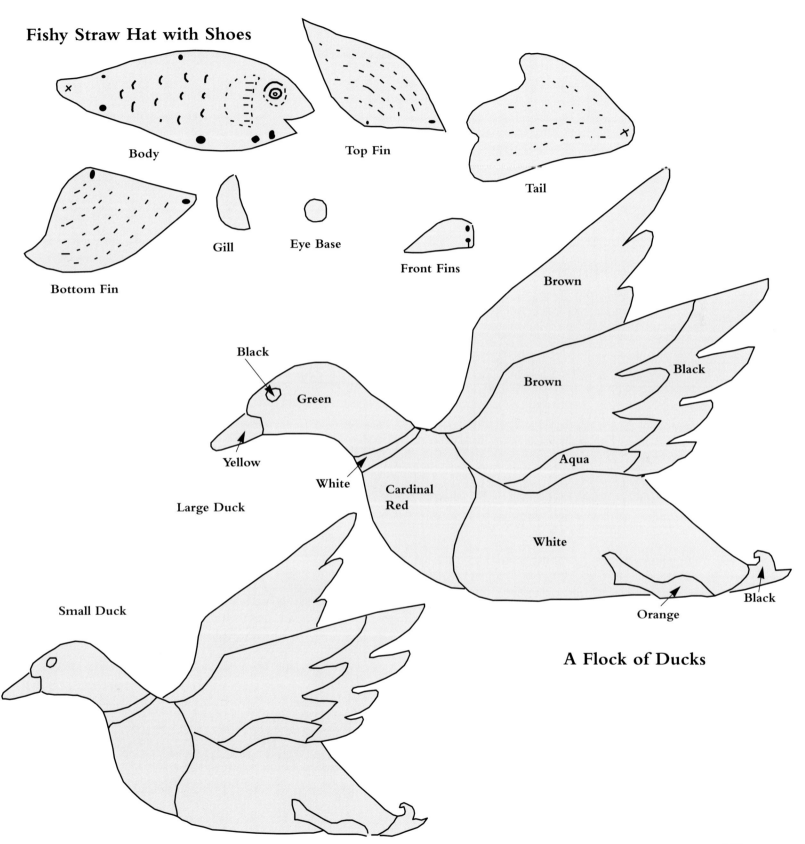

Fishy Straw Hat with Shoes

Body

Top Fin

Tail

Bottom Fin

Gill

Eye Base

Front Fins

Black

Green

Yellow

White

Large Duck

Small Duck

Brown

Brown

Black

Aqua

Cardinal
Red

White

Orange

Black

A Flock of Ducks

165

Forest Interlude
Enlarge at 125 Percent

Sources for Products

Specialized materials for each project used in this book are listed below by page number; these products should be widely available. For further information, contact the manufacturers at the addresses given at the bottom of the page.

Page 12: Stop Fraying glue: Aleene's, Division of Artis, Inc. HeatnBond fusible webbing: Therm O Web, Inc. Ribbon: C. M. Offray & Sons, Inc. **Page 15:** HeatnBond fusible webbing: Therm O Web, Inc. Tulip Treasures Brilliant Jewel fabric paint, Tulip Treasures Precious Metal fabric paint, Tulip Treasures Shake-On glitter: Tulip Productions. **Page 17:** Aleene's OK to Wash It fabric glue: Aleene's, Division of Artis, Inc. Ribbons: Lion Ribbon Co. **Page 19:** Pellon Wonder Under fusible webbing: Freudenberg Nonwovens. **Page 22:** Ribbon: C. M. Offray & Sons, Inc.. Hem N Trim fusible webbing: Dritz Corp. Cotton Ball charms: Creative Beginnings. **Page 25:** Silks and Dye-na-flow silk pigments: Rupert, Gibbon and Spider. Brushes: Loew-Cornell. Erasable marking pen: Dritz Corp. **Page 28:** Brass charms: Creative Beginnings. Enamel fabric paint, glitter: Jones Tones. Unique Stitch glue: W. H. Collins, Inc. **Page 31:** HeatnBond Ultra Hold fusible webbing: Therm O Web, Inc. **Page 34:** OK to Wash It fabric glue, Ultra fusible webbing: Aleene's, Division of Artis, Inc. **Page 40:** Brass charms: Creative Beginnings. HeatnBond fusible webbing: Therm O Web, Inc. Plexi 400 fabric paint: Jones Tones. **Page 43:** Marvy fabric marker: Uchida of America. Tulip Soft Sparkling Tints paint: Tulip Productions. **Page 46:** Brass charms: Creative Beginnings. **Page 48:** HeatnBond Oringinal No-Sew fusbile webbing: Thermo O Web, Inc. Metallic thread: Kreinik Mfg. Co. Tulip Colorpoint fabric paint, Tulip Glitter fabric paint: Tulip Productions. Marvy fabric marker: Urchida of America. Acrylic rhinestones: The Beadery Craft Products. Aleene's OK to Wash It fabric glue: Aleene's, Division of Artis, Inc. **Page 51:** Liquid Beads press and peel foil: Plaid Enterprises. HeatnBond Ultra Hold fusible webbing: Therm O Web, Inc. **Page 54:** Embroidery floss: The DMC Corp. **Page 56:** HeatnBond fusible webbing: Therm O Web, Inc. Tulip Slick fabric paint, Tulip Treasures Brilliant Jewel fabric paint: Tulip Productions. **Page 58:** Tulip Colorpoint Stitch paint: Tulip Productions. **Page 60:** Tulip Soft Covers-All fabric paint: Tulip Productions. **Page 62:** Tulip Covers-All fabric paint, Tulip Soft Metallics fabric paint, Tulip Glitter dimensional paint, Tulip Pearl dimensional paint, Tulip Slick fabric paint: Tulip Productions. **Page 66:** HeatnBond fusible webbing: Therm O Web, Inc. Tulip Treasures Brilliant Jewel fabric paint, Tulip Treasures Shake-On glitter: Tulip Productions. **Page 70:** Tulip Crystals fabric paint, Tulip Soft Sparkling Tints paint: Tulip Productions. Aleene's OK to Wash It fabric glue, Aleene's Transfer It transfer medium: Aleene's, Division of Artis, Inc. **Page 73:** Creatively Yours Fabric Plus fabric glue, Loctite Corp. Shiny Bright Green, Shiny Brown, Metallic Pure Gold fabric paint: Plaid Enterprises, Inc. **Page 76:** Fabric: Daisy Kingdom, Inc. Creatively Yours Fabric Plus fabric glue: Loctite Corp. Shiny Black fabric paint: Plaid Enterprises, Inc. Jewelry gems: The Beadery Craft Products. **Page 79:** Lace: Wimpole Street Creations. Creatively Yours Fabric Plus fabric glue: Loctite Corp. **Page 82:** Lunch tote: Bagworks, Inc. Shiny Black, Pearl Emerald Green, Pearl Garnet Red, Pearl Deep Purple, Pearl Yellow, Pearl Sapphire Gem fabric paint: Plaid Enterprises, Inc. **Page 84:** Tulip Soft Brush Top fabric paint: Tulip Productions. Marvy fabric marker: Uchida of America. **Page 88:** Aleene's Ultra fusible webbing: Aleene's, Division of Artis, Inc. Fashion Show dimensional paint: Plaid Enterprises, Inc. **Page 91:** Aleene's OK to Wash It fabric glue, Aleene's jewelry glue: Aleene's, Division of Artis, Inc. **Page 94:** Tulip Soft Covers-All fabric paint: Tulip Productions. Cotton Ball charms: Creative Beginnings. **Page 96:** Ribbons, laces, trims: St. Louis Trimming, Inc. Old World beads: The Beadery Craft Products. Super Glue Gel glue: Loctite Corp. Tack-It Over and Over temporary glue: Aleene's, Division of Artis, Inc. **Page 104:** Aleene's OK to Wash It fabric glue: Aleene's, Division of Artis, Inc. Battenburg doilies: Wimpole Street

Creations. **Page 107:** Karen's Kreations Krinkles gathered ribbon: Karen's Kreations. Aleene's OK to Wash It fabric glue: Aleene's, Division of Artis, Inc. **Page 110:** Neon ribbon: Wm. E. Wright Ltd. HeatnBond Original No-Sew fusible webbing: Therm O Web, Inc. Fray Check seam sealant: Dritz Corp. **Page 114:** Fashion beads: The Beadery Craft Products. Creatively Yours Fabric Plus fabric glue: Loctite Corp. Floss: The DMC Corp. **Page 117:** Brass charms: Creative Beginnings. HeatnBond fusible webbing: Therm O Web, Inc. **Page 120:** HeatnBond fusible webbing: Therm O Web, Inc. Rainbow felt: Kunin Felt Co. Tulip Shiny fabric paint, Tulip Treasures Brilliant Jewel fabric paint: Tulip Productions. **Page 124:** Creatively Yours Fabric Plus fabric glue: Loctite Corp. Pearl Champagne fabric paint: Plaid Enterprises, Inc. **Page 127:** Aleene's Transfer It transfer medium, Aleene's OK to Wash It fabric glue: Aleene's, Division of Artis, Inc. HeatnBond Original No-Sew fusible webbing: Therm O Web, Inc. Scribbles dimensional paints: Duncan Enterprises. Cotton Ball charms: Creative Beginnings. Acrylic gemstones: The Beadery Craft Products. **Page 134:** Dye-na-flow silk colors: Rupert, Gibbon and Spider. American Painter brush: Loew-Cornell. Americana acrylic paints: DecoArt. Friendly plastic sheets: American Art Clay Co., Inc. **Page 138:** Stickers: Mrs. Grossman's Paper Company. Aleene's OK to Wash It fabric glue: Aleene's, Division of Artis, Inc. **Page 140:** HeatnBond Original No-Sew fusible webbing: Therm O Web, Inc. **Page 143:** Iron-On flocking: Spencer's Zoo. Tulip Dimensional fabric paint: Tulip Productions. **Page 146:** Scribbles dimensional fabric paint: Duncan Enterprises. **Page 149:** Permalba acrylic colors, Betty Denton disposable palette: Martin/F Weber Co. Stylist 11 permanent pen #5: Yasutomo & Company. Heat resistant tape: Distlefink Designs, Inc.

Aleene's
Division of Artis, Inc.
Buellton, CA 93427

American Art Clay Co., Inc.
4717 W. 16th St.
Indianapolis, IN 46222

Bagworks, Inc.
3933 California Pkwy. East
Ft. Worth, TX 76119

The Beadery Craft Products
P.O. Box 178
Hope Valley, RI 02832

C. M. Offray & Sons, Inc.
Rte. 24, Box 601
Chester, NJ 07930-0601

Creative Beginnings
475 Morro Bay Blvd.
Morro Bay, CA 93442

Daisy Kingdom, Inc.
134 NW 8th Ave.
Portland, OR 97209

DecoArt
P.O. Box 386
Stanford, KY 40484

Distlefink Designs, Inc.
P.O. Box 24
Hawkins Road
South Britain, CT 06487

The DMC Corp.
10 Port Kearny
South Kearny, NJ 07032

Dritz Corp.
P.O. Box 5028
Spartanburg, SC 29304

Duncan Enterprises
5673 East Shields Ave.
Fresno, CA 93727

Freudenberg Nonwovens
Pellon Division
1040 Avenue of the Americas
New York, NY 10018

Jones Tones
68743 Perez Rd.
Suite D16
Cathedral City, CA 92234

Kreinik Mfg. Co.
9199 Reistertown Rd.
Suite 209B
Owings Mills, SD 21117

Kunin Felt Co.
A Foss Manufacturing Company
380 Lafayette Rd.
P.O. Box 5000
Hampton, NH 03843

Lion Ribbon Co.
Rte. 24, Box 601
Chester, NJ 07930

Loctite Corp.
1001 Trout Brook Crossing
Rocky Hill, CT 06067-3910

Loew-Cornell
563 Chestnut Ave.
Teaneck, NJ 07666-2490

Martin/F Weber Co.
2727 Southampton Rd.
Philadelphia, PA 19154

Mrs. Grossman's Paper Co.
77 Digital Dr.
Novato, CA 94949

Plaid Enterprises, Inc.
P.O. Box 7600
Norcross, GA 30091

Rupert, Gibbon and Spider
P.O. Box 425
Healdsburg, CA 95448

Spencer's Zoo
715 Walnut Dr.
Rio Dell, CA 95562

St. Louis Trimming, Inc.
5040 Arsenal St.
St. Louis, MO 63134

Therm O Web, Inc.
770 Glenn Avenue
Wheeling, IL 60090

Tulip Productions
A Division of Polymerics, Inc.
24 Prime Park Way
Natick, MA 01760

W. H. Collins, Inc.
21 Leslie Ct.
Whippany, NJ 07981

Wimpole Street Creations
P.O. Box 395
West Bountiful, UT 84087

Wm. E. Wright Trimming Ltd.
85 South St.
West Warren, MA 01092